ABOUT THE AUTHOR

After gaining a degree in Zoology, Jane Smith became a wildlife filmmaker for the BBC Natural History Unit and National Geographic. She won an Emmy for her work and has also appeared on BBC Radio 4's *Tweet of the Day*. She now creates wildlife art from her home on the west coast of Scotland to communicate her passion for the natural world.

JANE SMITH

COMMUNITY

People and Wildlife on the West Coast of Scotland

First published in 2025 by Birlinn Ltd
West Newington House
10 Newington Road
Edinburgh EH9 1QS

www.birlinn.co.uk

ISBN: 978 1 78027 935 0

British Library Cataloguing in Publication Data

A catalogue record for this book is available from the British Library

Designed and typeset in Arno Pro by Nye Hughes Studio

Printed and bound by Bell and Bain Ltd, Glasgow

Front cover illustration: *Creels and house sparrows*
Inside front and back covers: *Creel design*
Frontispeice: *Nesting Swallows*
Back cover: Detail from *Swifts flying*

Harris

St Kilda

North Uist

Scotland

Eigg

Loch Arkaig

Argyll Hope Spot

Knapdale

Islay

Glasgow

Dumfries

INTRODUCTION

I started this book as a celebration of communities of wildlife. In my twenties I used to make wildlife programmes. I filmed in landscapes all over the world and I fell in love with the beauty of ecosystems – communities of animals and plants, evolved together over millennia to live with each other and their surroundings. The complexity of these systems is mind-blowing. Every tiny animal has its own set of relationships, exploiting or being exploited, working together or in competition, to make perfect sustainable use of every element of the resources on offer. And every organism, no matter how small, plays a vital role in the overall community. For example, our Caledonian pine trees tolerate aphids feeding on their sugary sap. The aphids excrete the excess sugar, and this entices wood ants 30 metres up into the branches to 'milk' the aphid honeydew. Ants also need protein so they hunt other insects living in the tree. Thus the pine is protected from insect pests. It's an elegant community-based solution developed over thousands of years.

I wanted to learn more about the wildlife communities of the place I now live – the west coast of Scotland. I was excited, but also nervous. On my filming travels I've seen so many wild places depleted or destroyed by humans. Just 500 years ago Scotland was still a Garden of Eden for both humans and animals, with unpolluted water to drink, plentiful fish in the rivers, and vast forests providing food and shelter. Gradually the trees were cut down, either for fuel or to build warships or to clear space for farming. Two hundred years ago during the Clearances, landlords removed local small-scale farmers from the land and stocked it with sheep. The resulting bare mountainsides still surround us today. Would I find a landscape changed beyond the point of recovery? And would that even matter? We humans have learned to create our own ecosystems. Fossil fuels allow us to make artificial fertilisers, pesticides, herbicides and veterinary medicine to grow our own food independently of the natural world. Would I find that humans no longer need or value the natural world?

I encountered plenty of sheep-bitten hillsides, glens denuded of trees and sea-lochs polluted by industrial-scale fishfarms, but what I discovered also, surprised me. Traditionally this landscape degradation has been someone else's problem to

[opposite] *Locations of the projects visited*

solve: legislators, government departments or even the European Union. On my travels I encountered a growing number of human communities who are starting to take action: crofters, members of wildlife conservation charities, community landowners, and people so fed up of waiting for governments to do something that they have banded together to make change for themselves. The book became about these different communities of people as well as the wildlife communities they are restoring.

I grew up in the 1980s in a large town on the south coast of England. Politics at the time valued the individual over society. When I eventually settled in a small village in Argyll it took me a while to adjust to being part of a community. Baking cakes for a coffee-morning is still outside my comfort zone, but over the last 25 years I have learned how powerful it can be when people work together for the common good.

It's no surprise that community land ownership in the UK started on the west coast of Scotland. If you live on one of the many offshore islands, battered in winter (and even in summer) by storms, cut off from the mainland by dangerous seas, you really understand the value of community. Everyone is known for the skills that they provide to help their neighbours survive. In the modern world, our idea of community has expanded to a size that is no longer useful. Hollywood stars take on the characters that keep us company. But in the small village where I live, everyone is famous for something; there's the leader, the teacher, the grafter, the jester, the person who bakes cakes or who mends boats.

The west coast island of Eigg was one of the first Scottish communities to buy their island, back in 1997, followed in 2002 by the community purchase of the island of Gigha. As pioneers, it took them time to find their way, but now mainland communities are being inspired by their successes and are working to take ownership of the landscape in a moral as well as a legal way. This community environmental movement feels like the start of something exciting. We undoubtedly have a huge challenge ahead in the form of global warming and biodiversity loss, but I hope that by celebrating the work of these communities, more people will be inspired to make positive change. During the research for this book I have met so many people who have given up saying 'Something should be done,' and instead are asking 'What can we do?'

In order to learn more about the west coast of Scotland, I needed to find some experts. We all experience the world through the lens of our own knowledge. When I'm walking in the woods, I'm listening to the songs of different migrant birds. When I hear a wood warbler, freshly arrived from Africa, I know that spring has begun. My husband, Mark, a wildlife cameraman, might be noticing other things: the place where a badger has dug up bluebell bulbs to eat, or the plucking-post of a sparrowhawk. Both would provide good locations for filming. If my friend, a landscape archaeologist, joined us he might be seeing the way that trees have regrown after pollarding, indicating where an ancient field system was 150 years ago. However, we're all probably chatting about something completely different, just noticing our surroundings subconsciously, not giving our own knowledge any value because of its familiarity. Writing this book was a delight, as it gave me access to people who've spent a lifetime becoming an expert in something. I could pester them with questions, and they were all incredibly generous with their time and knowledge, allowing me to see the landscape in a new way.

And in true west coast fashion, my expectations were constantly subverted. For the first chapter on gardening, my idea was to find an ordinary garden owned by normal people. I met retired couple Roger and Annette, who seemed ordinary enough at first, but then, of course, turned out to be extraordinary. Quite apart from listening to Deep Purple and Rush at breakfast time and competing over their rival football teams (Aston Villa v. Hull), they taught me so much about my own county of Argyll. I've lived here for 25 years and thought I knew about it, but I was about to discover so much more.

JANE SMITH · MAY 2025

HOME

CHAPTER ONE

GARDEN

With thousands of miles of coastline, and mountains over 4,000 feet high, the landscape of the west of Scotland is a lot to get one's head around, so I decide to start my investigation in a smaller, more familiar version of the real thing – a garden. It's a mini-kingdom where each of us can create the ideal landscape for our own needs. Whenever I feel discouraged about the state of the natural world, I take refuge in the one place where I do have some influence. Having a garden is like having my own private nature reserve.

It's small, but with a lot of variety, which means it provides multiple resources in the one place. Sparrows nest under the eaves, hunt for hawthorn flies in the hedge and dust-bathe in bare patches on the driveway. Goldfinches raise their chicks in the yew tree next to my washing line and teach their youngsters to feed on thistles that we leave to go to seed. We let a patch of the lawn grow tall as a wildflower mini-meadow, and now slow worms winter in the thick thatch at the base. Mark scattered old roof tiles on the compost heap and delights in lifting them to find tangles of these golden legless lizards basking underneath. They have a beautiful gentle face and a tiny flickering tongue, and our daughter loves to lift them carefully and let them twine through her fingers.

A few years ago we dug a small pond. Well, I say we, but it was Mark with a spade and a wheelbarrow. We're still waiting for an otter to take a bath there, but on mild evenings it's a joy to hear the breeding frogs croaking away. Dragonflies discovered it in the first year and we have had fun identifying them. We watched a chocolate-lime southern hawker laying eggs in the damp moss at the edge. Delicate blue damselflies helicopter above the surface, and ugly larval monsters climb up the rosebay willowherb stalks to erupt out of their skin and fly free as four-spotted chasers. This process has given me hope for the future. If you give nature an opportunity it will recover. There are over 20 million gardens in the UK. If we all left the corners to go wild and grew insect-friendly flowers, we would have an enormous community nature reserve.

All habitats start at grass-roots level. In my garden, I learn about plants by weeding. Seeing the roots, the intimate parts that are normally hidden from view, you get a sense of the plant's personality. Wild strawberries are tough frontier characters, sending out wiry runners overland to colonise unpromising stony ground. The new plantlets have short roots but are supplied with water and nutrients by their parent while they establish themselves in new territory. They grow quickly into a low carpet of vegetation, creating their own microclimate. Buttercups send white grasping tentacles into the earth to search for water – very annoying if you're trying to pull them out. They don't need deep roots because their luxuriant leaf-growth shades the ground, stopping rainwater from evaporating. My favourite weeds are dandelions, even though they will probably be my downfall. Their single root grows vigorously downwards in search of water and anchors the plant, making its removal almost impossible. In fact every part of this plant is impressive in design. The arrow-like leaves curve up to catch the sun's rays for making energy. The sun-bright flowers are a food-source for bees. And then, the dandelion clock, a pale globe clustered perfectly into a sphere, packed with seeds at the centre. All that genetic information attached to featherlight lifting apparatus, allowing the rooted plant to send its children off on the wind – all over my garden!

Most gardeners try to keep the native plants (also known as weeds) at bay. They prefer to grow a curated community of plants, artificially persuaded to grow together despite having differing soil needs. Growing my own vegetables has made me realise how difficult this is. Courgettes like a soil rich in nutrients and lots of water. Kale likes some lime in the soil to make it alkaline, but blueberries grow best in acidic ground. Managing their different preferences brought it home to me that in the wild, plants grow in natural communities on the type of soil that sustains them. The land area covered by that soil limits each type of habitat. To understand the landscapes of the west coast, I need to start from the bottom and find out how rock and soil are created.

[opposite] *Dandelion and swifts*

I happen upon my perfect guides completely by accident. I first meet Roger and Annette Anderton when they buy one of my pictures. Whilst delivering it, I notice a teasel plant growing near their front door. Several bees are feeding on the purple flowers. Roger explains that the only place in the garden that they can grow teasels is right next to the house where lime mortar leaches out of the wall and makes the soil less acidic and so more fertile. When I show interest, I'm treated to a mass of fascinating information.

He explains that the house was built from a local greenish stone, metamorphosed basalt, but the dressings, the stonework around the windows and doors, were made from more easily cut sandstone. This dates the house to post-1835 when newly invented steam trains and steam ships allowed the transportation of sandstone from quarries near Glasgow. The basalt, however, has been used in Argyll for thousands of years, as it's soft enough to chisel but durable too. Most of the area's famous archaeological artefacts, like medieval grave slabs (500 years old), standing stones (3,000 years old) and cup-and-ring marks (5,000 years old) use this stone.

I'm delighted. Not only have I found a keen gardener, but also an historian who can shed light on how humans have affected this landscape. I quickly discover, however, that my timescale is out by a factor of over 600 million. The reason Roger is interested in basalt is because he's a geologist. He has retired from lecturing, but still has a youthful passion for geology. Because of the way he explains things, something I'd found dry and abstract at school is suddenly brought to life and made relevant. 'The continents are still moving,' he tells me, 'at the same speed that your toenails grow.' Once he gets going, so many fascinating bits of information tumble out of him that I have to return several times to check I've understood it all. I'll lay out the parts most relevant to our story here, with the proviso that, as theories are constantly evolving, this is our understanding so far. I've also simplified slightly, but even so, you might need to read the next page several times as geological time is a lot to take on.

[opposite] *Teasels and bumblebee*

13.8 Gya.*	The Big Bang creates the Universe.
4.5 Gya.	Debris and gases circling around our sun start to clump into planets, and our solar system is born.
4.4 Gya.	Water is delivered by icy asteroids (or it may have been here already). The surface of the earth becomes cool enough for the first rocks to form. The oldest rocks in the world include Lewisian gneiss, formed over 3 Gya and are still visible in north-west Scotland.
2.3 Gya.	Oxygen, produced by photosynthetic bacteria, starts to accumulate in the oceans, but does not yet move into the atmosphere.
1.8 Gya.	The cooling crust, 'floating' on denser rocks beneath, has clumped together into the first huge supercontinent. This acts like a blanket and the lava heats up underneath. The mantle eventually fissures about 1.5 Gya and the freed continents float off, to collide again elsewhere half a billion years later.
850 Mya.	Oxygen starts to escape into the atmosphere, building up to near present-day concentrations by 550 Mya, allowing the evolution of more complex organisms.
600 Mya.	By now the second supercontinent is breaking up. Where land masses collide, there is intense heat and pressure, mountain ranges are produced and some of the rocks (like the basalt from which the Andertons' house is built), are metamorphosed. Originally basalt, formed from molten magma, is black. Over the next 200 million years the actions of the moving continents push it 25 kilometres underground, where it heats to 500°C. The pressure and temperature change it chemically, and when it returns to the surface it is green.
420 Mya.	Scotland, as part of a bigger land mass, collides with England. At this time the first land plants are appearing. They remove carbon dioxide from the atmosphere, which cools it, but other influences like volcanic eruptions, heat it.
66 Mya.	An asteroid collides with the earth, causing tidal waves and fires, and sends so much dust into the atmosphere that most land animals heavier than 25kg could no longer survive. Most of the dinosaurs, having evolved for 165 million years, become extinct in just a few years.

60 Mya.	North America detaches from Scotland and heads westward, leaving a chain of extinct volcanoes in the Hebrides and creating the North Atlantic Ocean in its wake.
2.6 Mya.	The last ice age begins. Since 0.8 Mya there have been ice advances from the poles approximately every 100,000 years. ('You could set your watch by it,' says Roger.) This is controlled by features of the Earth's motion around the sun.
300 Kya.	Humans (*Homo sapiens*) evolve in Africa.
20 Kya.	The last glacial advance. The ice gouges out the rock, cutting the glens and long sea lochs that form the west coast now.
12 Kya.	As the ice melts, small groups of humans arrive in Scotland, living off the land.

* *Gya is a billion years ago, Mya is a million years ago and Kya is a thousand years ago. A billion is a thousand millions!*

To give some perspective, if all the text in this book represented time since the Big Bang, the last 10,000 years, when humans arrived in Scotland and geology became history, would be a fraction of the final full stop. It's mind-blowing. I find this geological perspective strangely comforting. When I drive up the west coast and see massive hillsides that have been there for billions of years, it puts my own problems into perspective.

My conversations with Roger make me realise how much geology pushes evolution forwards. When the continents collided, the coasts were cool and damp, but away from the sea, in the centre of the huge land mass, there was no water, and animals were forced to adapt to the desert conditions. Today geology still controls the weather. The high mountains above Fort William force the damp Atlantic winds to rise, cool and drop their rain straight away, whereas the flatter Kintyre peninsula allows clouds to pass over and reach Glasgow before they drop their load.

Geology also controls where we live and how our human communities operate. Over millennia, the multi-layer rock sandwich, beneath what is now Argyll, folded and then rose to the surface. The tops of the folds eroded, exposing strips of rock only a few kilometres wide. 'I love living here,' Roger tells me, 'because the rock structure makes the landscape so varied.' In Argyll rich limestone fields nestle up to wood-covered hills and craggy moorlands. Farming is small-scale and varied, and communities are composed of rural villages or coastal fishing towns.

Ten thousand years ago, Scotland was covered in ice. As it gradually receded, the ground was exposed to the warming sun. Rock had been fractured by ice and ground down under the glaciers, creating soil from different minerals. Plants moved in, evolving to survive on the different soil types. Insects evolved to pollinate the plants, and animals to feed on or shelter under them.

The chapters of this book are based around ten different wildlife communities: woodland, river, peatland etc. However, as I travelled up the west coast I discovered that the most interesting part of this story was the way that these wildlife communities were intertwined with communities of people.

When I told my friends I was getting into gardening there were comments about becoming old and boring. But you should never conflate those two characteristics, and neither should you ever underestimate a gardener. While I sit in the sun asking Roger about geology, his wife, Annette, pours the tea and passes the biscuits. Now I'm going to introduce you to her, because she gives us the next part of this story. She proves that you don't need to be a big landowner to take part in 'rewilding', and you can have a positive effect on international wildlife populations from your own garden.

During our conversation I notice swallows and house martins swooping after insects around the tall sycamores; but suddenly we are interrupted by a party of screaming swifts. These mysterious birds are rare in Argyll. I've seen them in Mediterranean cities, racing low over the rooftops in noisy flocks, screaming to each other in high-speed chase, then at dusk circling higher and higher until they disappear from view, to sleep on the wing. They've been seen from aeroplanes at 30,000 feet. Their long scimitar wings are perfect for life in the upper air.

Annette explains that when she and Roger moved into their house, they weren't expecting to share it with swifts. One day when doing the ironing upstairs, she saw one flying at speed straight towards the window. It vanished, and she realised it was nesting in a hole under the roof. A few months later, when clearing the gutters, they found a dead swift, stuck in the hole. The roof of a neighbouring building had recently been repaired, and it could have been that local birds were searching

[opposite] *Swifts flying*

for alternative accommodation. Annette decided to take action and researched swift nest boxes to install under the eaves. Her first boxes, in 2015, had a hole at the front, and the local starlings moved straight in. Luckily they had fledged their first brood by May, and when the swifts arrived they took over. However they were continually harassed by the starlings, so in 2017 Annette decided to design her own box with a long narrow entrance underneath. The swifts installed themselves and, delighted to have such exotic tenants, Annette would wait for ages by the bedroom window for the birds to return with food for their chicks. In 2018, to learn even more (and to avoid getting a crick in her neck) she installed cameras inside two boxes.

Nesting swifts are unusual on the west coast of Scotland because they feed on airborne insects. Most of our air is blown in from the Atlantic and insects are rare out at sea. We're not known for our dry climate either, and insects are often rained out of the air. However our landscape is either wild or is farmed for animals, both of which can produce good insect life.

Swifts are real specialists. Their long narrow wings allow them to fly fast enough to escape any aerial predator, but don't provide much lift. If they land on the ground they struggle to take off again. The benefits and disadvantages of this wing-shape have pushed swifts into a life lived for most of the year high above the earth. They rarely use their legs, which are very short, and their scientific name, 'Apus', means 'without feet'. They've learned to do everything on the wing. They skim, beak open, across lake surfaces to drink and bathe. They mate in the air and gather nesting material from the wind. Their forked tails can be folded and tapered for speed, or flared out when turning. Their eyes are deep-set for protection when traveling at high speed. When food becomes scarce in bad weather, they can fly hundreds of miles around weather systems to find the sun-warmed air which lifts their prey high into the sky. Swifts prefer nest holes in tall buildings where they have enough height to drop into flight-speed. Modern houses have sealed roof-spaces, and the main limit to swift populations in the UK is availability of nest sites. Between 1995 and 2016 we have lost more than half our swift population.

When the swifts arrive, they fly past their nest holes, banging them with their wing tips. 'A bit like children running down the street banging on the front doors to show off to their friends,' says Annette. There's no official explanation for this behaviour. It may be a demonstration of flying skill. It may be to check if the box is already occupied, as it provokes the resident couple to go to the entrance and 'duet scream'. It may be to dislodge any squatters. It's safer than looking in and getting jabbed in the face by a starling.

When Annette and Roger had scaffolding erected for the repair of their roof, the starlings perched below the new nest boxes and, after diligent practice, worked out how to enter through the narrow gap. Annette now seals the hole until May when swifts return. She and Roger must then heave a 7-metre ladder into position and climb up to the eaves to open the boxes – true dedication to the cause.

Annette had worked as a microbiologist, and so was familiar with scientific process. She read everything she could find, including the book *Swifts in a Tower* about a 75-year study of birds nesting at Oxford University. She upgraded her first grainy black-and-white cameras to higher resolution, and became fascinated with the lives of her avian tenants. The spare bedroom became Swift HQ, and Annette invites me to come and draw the birds from the monitors. The swifts are in darkness, but we can see them, as the cameras work with infra-red light. It's such a privilege to witness the intimate moments of the birds' lives – from their excitement in May when the pair greet each other on returning from eight months of travelling, to the day in early August when their last chick tumbles scrambling into the outside world and successfully fledges. The birds build their nest in the darkest corner, a huge contrast to their lives in the bright expanse of sky. They bring in wind-blown feathers, grass, flowers and once even a butterfly, which they glue together with sticky threads of saliva. This hardens in air to hold the nest together. (Some species of swift use only their saliva, and these nests are collected to make the Chinese delicacy Birds' Nest Soup.)

Each spring Annette and Roger make sure the nest boxes are properly clean and free of any parasites or their eggs. As well as the usual burden of uninvited guests (lice, mites and fleas), swifts have their own parasite, called a swift louse-fly, *Crataerina pallida*. These pallid spidery wingless flies are blood-sucking insects which survive over winter as a chrysalis. They hatch at about the same time as the swift chicks, and look comparatively huge. If swifts were human-size it would be like having several crabs scuttling around under your clothes and sucking your blood. Annette shudders just telling me about them.

Some scientific studies mark individual birds to tell them apart, but Annette doesn't want to risk doing that, as swifts have been known to desert the nest when disturbed. As the birds are not only site-faithful but box-faithful, she is confident in identifying the pairs, which usually mate for life, but as the sexes look the same, she can't identify male from female. Each year one member of the pair in box one always arrives later than its mate, sometimes by ten days. It seems that the early bird (an egg-layer so therefore female) may conduct other liaisons while waiting, as the season starts with marital strife, the jealous partner throwing the first-laid egg out of the box. They eventually agree on two eggs, and fledge two chicks by August.

In July 2019 a new pair of birds installed themselves in box two. A popular myth is that once juvenile birds fledge, they don't land for four years until they're ready to breed. However, Annette realised that these must be prospecting youngsters. For three years they don't lay eggs, but practise being homeowners. 'They are delightful, cosying up together and preening each other, like teenagers in love,' she tells me. In 2022 this pair arrived in mid-May, six weeks earlier than their usual date. They laid three eggs, which would be rare in England, but especially so in a Scottish summer when a week of rain can make insects hard to come by. I couldn't visit, as Annette and Roger were shielding from Covid, but I received regular updates on WhatsApp. Annette was worried that the young and inexperienced pair wouldn't cope with raising three chicks, but all the eggs hatched and she sent me a photo of the 'three ugly little dinosaurs'. Then, as if the stress was too much, one of the parents disappeared for three days. The remaining adult became infected with louse-flies, presumably from visiting another nest site. It lay panting next to the begging chicks, exhausted. Annette was distraught, but at this point she had to leave, to look after her mother who was seriously ill. 'I left with a heavy heart,' she told me, 'fearing not only for my Mum, but also for the swifts. When I got home, the first thing I did was go and turn on the cameras. I was feeling quite sick, and expected to see a heap of dead bodies.' To her delight, both adults were present and had been able to find enough food for their three offspring.

[opposite] *Fully-grown swift chicks*

Annette records fantastic video footage to keep me updated with progress. By July the chicks are almost as big as their parents. At night the adults still try to brood their youngsters, all of them cramming into a corner on top of each other for maximum body contact, even though the babies can spend all night fidgeting. The adults aren't early risers, but wait for the day to warm and the insects to fly. They can feed their chicks every ten minutes or as little as every two days in bad weather, the chicks going into a torpor to survive until conditions improve. We watch the adults return with bulging throats full of insects stuck together with saliva into a ball. When the chicks are young this gets divided, but at this stage one chick can get the whole lot. I have sympathy for the adults who are mobbed by their ravenous young, attacking until food is regurgitated.

One of the best bits is watching the youngsters doing press-ups, lifting their bodies off the ground to strengthen their wing muscles for flight. They also flutter like a toy with a rubber-band motor. And then one day Annette sends me a video of a chick looking out of the hole and getting up its courage, like a child gearing up to dive off the high board. Finally it launches out into thin air, never to return to its nest. It will head south to Africa, living on the wing until it returns to Scotland in a year's time.

In future years most of the youngsters will look for a different colony in another house to avoid interbreeding. That's why it's important to put up more boxes. Outside the house we count 16 swifts from the local area, circling overhead. Swifts can't be protected with nature reserves, but need help from people like Annette. She's been advising her neighbours, who've asked how to put up boxes on their own houses. Some people are worried about potential mess, but she reassures them that, unlike house martins, swifts are tidy and don't leave their droppings everywhere.

Fortified by Annette's enthusiasm for wildlife, and informed by Roger's basic introduction to geology, I feel that I'm ready to explore some wilder parts of the Scottish landscape. I decide to head off in my van to see if I can make sense of the bigger picture.

[opposite] *Goldfinches on thistles*

WESTERN ISLES

CHAPTER TWO

PEATLAND

One of the largest peat bogs in Europe is on the Isle of Lewis in the Outer Hebrides. Peatlands have been accumulating there for many thousands of years, and are interwoven with the culture of the Hebridean people. The rest of Scotland has long seen peatlands as a barren wilderness on the margins of the country, but recently that has all changed. The discussion about global warming has set peatlands at the centre of a very modern and important debate.

Lewis and Harris are one island, split historically by belonging to two different clans. To reach the island I have to cross the Sound of Harris. It's eight miles of racing tides and is my favourite ferry crossing in the world. At 7am I'm surprised to find the ferry full of beautifully dressed youngsters, the boys in traditional kilt, jacket, waistcoat and tie, even down to the ribbon flashes in their socks. The girls have immaculate French braids which means they must have got out of bed a lot earlier than me. Their parents are crowding around the coffee machine chatting in the local Gaelic, so there's a vacant front seat by the picture window. My neighbour tells me the excursion is for a piping competition on Harris. People here are fiercely proud of their heritage.

As we head out, we pass a red marker-buoy with a cluster of black guillemots roosting aboard, their bright red feet matching the paintwork. They scatter as we approach, joining the rafts of eider ducks bobbing on the rough water. It's gusting 30 knots but the Sound is so shallow that there's no swell. A profusion of buoys, half red, half green, are scattered amongst the islands. I'm wishing I had a travel companion with whom to make bets on where the ferry will head next. Maritime convention is to pass to the right of any red buoy as you leave port, although there are so many dotted about that guessing the route is almost impossible. We slalom through the markers, sometimes pirouetting and doubling back on ourselves. Gannets plunge dive in the turquoise rip-tide and then head off west to feed their waiting chicks on St Kilda. Delicate terns race past into the wind. A fin cuts through the waves and vanishes – a dolphin. After half an hour we must be on the approach to port, as we start to pass green buoys on the left. We pass eight sheep on a tiny island – no fences needed here.

As we near the Harris shore, I start to see red-throated divers flying past. These birds nest on the banks of the peaty lochans in the hills. On an island where everything from the outside world has to arrive by sea or air, resources are limited. This increases the sense of community but also, as I'm about to learn, makes life more complicated. I drive my van to a beautiful campsite on the beach where I've booked to stay a few nights. It's the end of the day, and when the owner comes to take my money, he's happy to stand and chat. He explains that his biggest problem is finding staff. Tourism provides vital income for the islands, but when houses are used for holidays it leads to a shortage of housing for local young people. Many leave for the mainland to find jobs. Local restaurants have closed because they can't find waiters, and Brexit compounded the problem. Inspired by the success of other islands, like the Isle of Eigg, local people have started to take ownership of their own landscape to solve their problems. They want to build affordable houses and also to manage their landscape in a sustainable way. I arrange to speak to one of their organisations, the Carloway Estate Trust, but first I want to learn more about peat, and to see Lewis' most famous landmark.

I visit the Callanish Stones on an atmospheric, dreich day, with curlews calling from the moors. This stone circle, standing high on a ridge in the peatlands, is visible from land and sea for miles around. The stones were erected in Neolithic times, earlier than the more famous Stonehenge monument, and were used as a focus for ritual activity into the Bronze Age. In the 5,000 years that they've stood here in wind and rain, peat slowly accumulated around them until the smaller stones all but disappeared from view. Now they've been excavated to their original height. I'd heard that in the seventeenth century the people of the islands took to calling the stones 'fir bhrèige', false men, who were turned to stone for refusing to listen to the word of Christ. If you're being literal, the Lewisian gneiss rocks were turned to stone well over a billion years ago, and erected here a mere 3,000 years before the birth of Christ. But when I stood amongst them they did feel like people: characters with a different perspective on time from our own. They helped me gain a perspective on the ancient peatland.

[opposite] *Nesting curlew*

So how is peat formed? Most plants use nutrients from rock as building-blocks for growth. The plants convert minerals into living biological matter, which at the end of each year decays to create soil. However, Lewisian gneiss doesn't break down easily, as evidenced by the longevity of the Callanish stones. Many plants can't survive on such meagre fare, but sphagnum moss can gain enough nutrients just from rainwater. A plentiful supply of this arrives when the prevailing westerly winds, thick with moisture from their journey across 3,000 miles of Atlantic Ocean, make landfall in the Outer Hebrides. The moss controls its environment by holding on to this water – as anyone who has tried sitting on a clump of sphagnum will know to their cost! The waterlogged conditions prevent competition from other plants, as they stop oxygen reaching down into the soil. Only plants with specific adaptations can survive. Cottongrass, the plant with fluffy white tufts that cover the peatlands in summer, has air channels in its leaves that allow air to travel right down to its roots.

Like all plants, sphagnum moss harnesses the energy from sunlight to break down carbon dioxide. It discards the oxygen (which we breathe) and uses the carbon to build its cells. Normally bacteria in the soil would decompose dead vegetation and return the carbon into the air. On a bog the cold temperatures and lack of oxygen in the waterlogged soil mean that plants don't fully decay, but instead form peat, locking the carbon into the ground. Peat bogs are thus a vital weapon in the fight against global warming.

But on an island without trees, they have also been used for centuries as a source of fuel. Over millions of years, when continents collided, heat and pressure turned peat into coal, but island people discovered that a much simpler way to get energy was to burn the peat itself. The smell of a peat fire still represents home to many Hebridean folk. Many crofters in the Western Isles have a peat bank where they cut and dry enough peat for the winter. I went to visit my friend Ruth, and offered to help her 'at the peats'. As with many traditional jobs, it's labour-intensive, but also a great way to be outside and experience the peatland. As we pick our way carefully across the boggy ground the mournful cry of a golden plover reaches us – it must have chicks nearby.

[opposite] *Golden plover and peat stacks*

Spotted chaser dragonflies and bog plants

Ruth, despite being almost 80, stacks peat for her neighbour and herself. The wind whistles in the holes of her NHS-issue walking sticks, and she has tied plastic bags around her feet as they are currently too sore for wellies. Several people here have told me that youngsters nowadays don't know what hard work is. Working with Ruth, I have to agree. The job will take her many days; she sums it up as eat, sleep, re-peat. At night, when I'm sleeping in my van outside her house and she's awake with the pain in her legs, she continues our daytime conversations online. She was born in Wales and I'd asked her about learning Gaelic. 'I mainly learnt and got fair fluency by listening to Radio nan Gael when I was out at peats, going back 20 years to when I was learning to hand-cut them with old Willie as mentor,' she writes.

Traditionally the brick-sized peats are cut with a tairsgeir, a special peat-iron made by the local blacksmith. The face of the peat bank can be five feet deep. Cutting down into history, the soil becomes darker, softer, changing from the colour of cheap milk chocolate to that of luxury Belgian truffle. Fresh, sodden peat is heavy and needs two hands to turn a block, but these blocks have been drying for several months and are light enough to carry in a pile. We heap them into a 'rudhan' or stack, to dry some more in the wind. As we work, we do mental arithmetic, working out what percentage we have gathered and what there is still left to do – until we realise this is demoralising, and chat to take our minds off it. I wonder if, in terms of global warming, it must be better to burn a local carbon source like peat, rather than import fossil fuels? Ruth agrees, and also reminds me that a much bigger issue is commercial harvesting of peat for garden compost.

The problem with peat-cutting is that the exposed bank can allow water to drain out, drying the bog. This allows the peat to decompose, releasing carbon dioxide which increases global warming. But now as renewable energy becomes an option, the community is faced with new dilemmas. Recently there have been proposals to install megawatt wind farms on the peatlands. Does this matter? Maybe these wide-open spaces have no value for the next generation if young people no longer do manual labour on the moors. None of this is straightforward.

As we walk back to the van I find a meadow pipit's nest of pale woven grass under a tussock with four miniature mottled eggs inside. With few nutrients available, peatland plants aren't big and showy, but small and inventive. Bejewelled red sundews use sticky sap to trap insects for extra nourishment. So do purple butterwort, so-called because the digestive enzymes in its yellow star-shaped leaves are traditionally used to curdle milk.

Another speciality of the peatlands is the red-necked phalarope. Most of this bird's population breed in the Arctic, but a few breed in the Outer Hebrides. Bird-nerd that I am, I'm keen to see them. I set up my telescope on a calm evening on the shore of a peat lochan where I'm told they breed. I wait an hour, checking every small bird that flies past. Eventually I spot two dainty birds, swimming and darting after insects. They pirouette on the water surface to make tiny whirlpools which bring food to the surface. Unlike most birds, it is the male phalarope who incubates the eggs and cares for the chicks. Once she has laid the clutch, the female will head back out to the ocean.

The colours in the evening light are muted and remind me of Harris Tweed: greens, greys and flecks of orange. In the past, local plants were collected to dye wool, and a lichen called crottle was used to create those flecks of orange and red. It also gave a distinctive scent to the tweed, possibly because urine was saved by the crofters and used as a mordant to fix the dye. The production of Harris tweed is another traditional skill that takes time and hard labour. To receive the official orb stamp, Harris Tweed must be pure Scottish wool, dyed and spun by the islanders of the Outer Hebrides and woven by hand in their home. Local wool is incredibly hard-wearing and great protection against wind and rain, but also rough on the skin. To make it more suitable for the fashion industry, local fleeces are sent away to be blended with softer wool from the Scottish mainland. To find out more I pay a visit to Donald MacDonald who welcomes tourists in the weaving shed behind his house. The air has an old-fashioned smell of wool and machinery grease. I ask him how many years he's been weaving Harris Tweed and he laughs, 'Since God was a boy.'

He learned on this same loom, his father's, and at 16 started work for a mill in Stornoway. Like most islanders he has had several jobs, giving up the weaving every so often when he needs a change. He's also had to fit in the croft work, and I can see

[opposite] *Red-necked phalaropes*

his sheep grazing in the field by the house. But now he has a pension, he does the weaving for his own enjoyment. He makes his own designs, inspired by a lifetime knowledge of pattern, and by the colours he sees around him. It reminds me a lot of my screen printing, where a combination of colours will start off a picture.

The weaving begins with tying 672 knots for the warp threads that will run the length of the fabric. And then, as Donald moves the foot pedals, the shuttle fires across the loom with a loud clack to pull through the wool that makes up the horizontal weft. It can be dangerous if the shuttle breaks free, and there are dents in the wall to prove it. Different colours create patterns in the fabric, and it strikes me that the tweed could be a metaphor for the peatland ecosystem. All the threads contribute to the integrity of the piece. If a small hole appears at the edge of the cloth it can be darned, but if one thread is removed it affects the strength of the whole piece.

It takes three weeks to make a length of tweed: one week to dye and spin the yarn, one to weave, and one to wash and dry it. This last part was done by 'waulking', when the women beat the cloth and sang songs to create a rhythm and make the work pass quicker. This is now done by machine in the factory, and Donald worries whether the younger generation will have the patience and perseverance enough to maintain other parts of the process. 'They're too busy with this,' and he wiggles his fingers on an imaginary computer keyboard. His Hattersley loom is 70 years old and he can no longer get spare parts. 'I remember when there were 28 of these looms working every day between here and the road end,' he says. 'Now there are fewer than 50 left in the Western Isles.' Today, tweed has become a luxury brand. Cloth from the islands is shipped to London, Paris and Tokyo. Fashion designers value its tradition and create a modern twist by ordering it in new colours. It's even been used by Nike in their trainers.

The depopulation of the islands started 200 years ago with the Clearances. Crofters were evicted by the landowners, who wanted to use the land for farming, and many families emigrated to Canada or Australia to look for work. Even in the last 50 years the population of Harris has halved, as young people leave to study or find a job that involves less hard physical labour. But it was an incomer who came up with a way to stem this tide. Entrepreneur Anderson 'Burr' Bakewell was born in America, but has made the Hebrides his home. 'Harris has given me a great deal over the past 40-odd years,' Mr Bakewell says. 'It's an opportunity for me to put something back.' He realised that production of a single-malt whisky would provide a business that lasted for generations, and would benefit from the island's strengths of patience and sense of community. Furthermore, if the essence of the island could be bottled and sent all over the world, tourists would be inspired to visit for their holidays, providing further income.

The small island of Pabbay was the last location where Harris whisky was produced, hidden away from the excisemen. In 1846 islanders were cleared from the land, emigrating to Cape Breton, and the island is now uninhabited. But the modern distillery needed to be somewhere more central. Bakewell found investors to fund a distillery in the village of Tarbert, and in 2015 the business was launched with a ceilidh in the newly built warehouse. In the 2011 census the island population had dropped to 1,916 individuals. The first release of 1,916 bottles was pre-sold to celebrate every individual within the community.

When I visit for a distillery tour in June 2023, the whisky has been maturing for eight years, and the company is preparing to release the first bottles in a few months. Our tour is led by a local lass whose aunts, uncles and cousins all work in the distillery. She tells us that in 2015 the business started with ten employees and with the ambition to double that in five years, but already there are more than 50 people working in sustainable jobs. While the whisky matures, the business is sustained by the production of Isle of Harris gin, which is much quicker to make. Flavoured with island botanicals and hints of sugar-kelp seaweed, this clear spirit is sold in a beautiful bluish bottle: colours of the turquoise sea and Hebridean sky.

The amber whisky, in contrast, is all about the land. We learn how Scottish barley is sprouted (malted) to release plant sugars, and then dried in the smoke of a peat fire to add flavour. The barley is mashed, soaked in water from a local stream and fermented with yeast in huge vats called washbacks. The delicious rich yeasty smell bubbles out of these cylinders to fill the room. Fermentation lasts between three and five days. A shorter time gives nuttier flavours and a longer time produces a fruitier taste. The resulting liquid is a type of beer which is then concentrated in custom-made copper stills to an alcohol strength of 68 per cent. We get to sample

this fiery liquor, which tastes amazing in itself, but this needs to mature for at least eight years before it can be called whisky. It is matured in oak casks that have previously been used to make either sherry in Spain or bourbon in Kentucky. The barrels rest in the oceanic climate of the west coast of the island, prevented from freezing by the Gulf Stream but cool enough to allow only a slight evaporation through the wood. This loss is known as the 'angels' share' and it also contributes to the final taste. Before bottling, the casks are blended to produce the distinctive flavour of The Hearach. This is the Gaelic word for a native of Harris, and is the name proudly chosen for their whisky. The bottle, like Harris gin, is inspired by the rippling lines of water on the strand, but these lines are straighter in homage to the warp and weft of the tweed. The H logo on the Hearach bottle is made from the figures of a distiller and crofter shaking hands, which symbolises the sense of community. The boxes have photos of local people, and each batch has tasting notes written by an islander and linked to island experience.

The left-over malt is called draff, and is sent to local farms to feed livestock. Employees are given paid service days to volunteer for social projects like beach cleans, and the company sponsors the Harris Football Club. In September 2023 the first bottles of the Hearach went on sale with a huge launch party and ceilidh in Tarbert. Many young people, who would otherwise have left the island, have stayed to work in a job that gives them great pride.

Before I leave Harris I'm booked to film for a TV series called *Painting Birds* with artist Jim Moir, aka comedian Vic Reeves. I don't know what to expect from a famous celebrity, but in real life, because he's an enthusiastic birdwatcher and artist, he seems perfectly normal to me. He and his co-presenter wife, Nancy Sorrell, want to have a go at screen printing in my campervan. I'm a bit nervous whether there will be enough room to make artwork, and it's a tight squeeze with cameraman, sound recordist and presenters, but we manage. They put an extra camera in the roof and also film through an open window. The morning rushes past. Jim wants to know why I choose to draw birds, and my answer relates to habitats. If you make a list of

[opposite] *Dunlin display*

the birds that live here, red-necked phalarope, red-throated diver, meadow pipit and hen harrier, then you sum up the peatlands. For me there's also an emotional connection too. Birds fly, and watching them allows me to imagine that freedom.

The sky-dancing display of hen harriers is only a recent spectacle over the peatlands of Lewis. Watching the male dive and swoop on a rollercoaster path through the sky is exhilarating. It was thought they wouldn't breed here because voles, one of their main prey species, don't occur on the island. However, recent community land purchases and changes in land management have coincided with a return, and when I visit, ten pairs are breeding. With fewer grazing sheep, the taller heather provides safer nest sites and more meadow pipits for prey. When bringing food back to the nest the male calls to summon the incubating female. She flies upside down to grab the prey mid-air in her talons.

Hen harriers are killed on sporting estates throughout England and Scotland, as they can eat the young grouse which are bred for shooting. In the nineteenth century they were driven to extinction in mainland Britain. They made their way back in the 1960s, but continue to be heavily persecuted. They have retreated to the margins of the country, and this is why their appearance on Lewis is such good news. Local ornithologists are attaching radio trackers to the chicks before they fledge, to help understand potential causes of death. It may also act as a deterrent to birds disappearing in suspicious circumstances.

The importance of peatlands has varied widely over the years. When peat was the only source of fuel and the community worked together to harvest it, it was important both culturally and practically. It also provided summer grazing on the sheilings, when women accompanied their livestock onto the moors. When fossil fuel became available for heating, and flights to the Mediterranean provided more exciting holidays, peatland lost its value. Its charms lie in the details: the song of the skylark, the smell of the heather and the tiny bright flowers. From a distance peatland seems like a drab forbidding place, and in the twenty-first century its low value has ironically given it a new importance – as a site for wind farms.

[opposite] *Hen harrier food pass*

The story of peatland provides fascinating dilemmas. Can it help solve the twin crises of climate change and biodiversity loss, while providing community prosperity? In 2004 a corporate conglomerate applied for planning permission to build 234 wind turbines on the Lewis peatland. Although local jobs were promised and green energy is vital, many people felt that their landscape was being taken away from them. They successfully fought off the development by weaving together cultural elements, poetic, historic and folkloric, into a speckled tweed as rich as the peatlands themselves. They published a glossary of peat-specific terms, called *Rathad an Isein* (*The Bird's Road*). This 'road' is the narrow gap left between the top edge of the peat bank and the row of cut peats which have been laid down to dry in the sun – narrow so only a bird could run along it as it forages for insects. This project highlighted the fact that if the vocabulary is lost, so is the relationship with the landscape. It lists sayings such as 'Sileadh e a-nis' (it can rain now), which expresses relief when the dried peats have been brought in from the hill. 'Lèig-chruthaich' is a crust of vegetation over water, something that you must be aware of if you don't want to break through it and soak yourself before a day of work on the moor.

More recently, a new wind-farm application has been approved with much greater community benefit built into the project. The Stornoway Wind Farm is to be built on land owned and managed on behalf of the community. The 36 turbines will have up to 20 per cent community ownership.

Everyone agrees that green energy is essential for our future survival, but wind turbines also have negatives. Large birds like golden eagles and hen harriers have been killed by the rotating blades. Before the new wind farm can be built, bird surveys will be undertaken to guide the placement of turbines away from breeding sites and hunting grounds. On the positive side, income streams from energy generation can help revitalise communities. In 2015 the Carloway Estate was bought by its local community to see if they could install their own turbines. They also discovered that there was funding available to restore their peatlands.

Peatlands are valuable for soaking up rainwater to prevent floods and to filter drinking water. Ben Inglis-Grant is the Carloway Peatland Action officer. One of his first jobs was to repair the peat bog that filtered the water supply of 3,500 islanders. Drains and peat cutting in the bog had allowed erosion to occur, drying out the peat soil, cracking and crumbling it and so adding sediment to the water. Restoring the surface of the bog kept the peat hydrated and the soil intact, preventing production of sediment which would otherwise release its stored carbon dioxide. There is more carbon stored in peatlands than in all the world's forests, and it's vital to keep it there. So should peat-cutting be banned? Crofters have the historic right to cut peat which is enshrined in law, but nowadays it's so much easier to flick a switch for clean energy. Electricity involves no smoke and no back-breaking work. One local tells me 'Peat-cutting is in decline. No-one's going to try and ban it. It's more likely that we'll be trying to preserve it for its cultural significance.'

On my way to the ferry I return for a last look at the Callanish Stones. The false men don't look very contrite to me. They've stood here for 5,000 years and will likely stand the same number of years again. The tall, skinny one seems to be looking down his nose, the broad one is shrugging his shoulders, and there's an accusing one with a raised pointy finger. The central stone looms above me as if in judgement. There's a west coast saying, 'When God made time, he made plenty of it'. Standing amongst these stones, I understand this properly. But at the same time, we are running out of time to avert climate disaster. Climate change won't bother the stone men – it's us who need to sort out this complicated but vital issue.

NORTH UIST

CHAPTER THREE

MACHAIR

I catch the ferry south down the chain of the Outer Hebrides to North Uist. It is a windy place, and I pass cottages with washing lines of clothes flapping in the gale. I head the few miles to the west coast, where long sandy beaches protect the island from the pounding waves of the Atlantic. The mountains behind me force the sea-wind skywards, and I can see a golden eagle soaring the up-draughts. It hangs in the breeze, then tucking back its wings, dives steeply. There's a blizzard of black and white wings as oystercatchers pipe their outrage and alarm and the eagle retreats upwards, talons empty. From its viewpoint on high it can see the whole island. On the coast the white shell-sand makes the sea glow turquoise, while inland, the dark, peaty ground is speckled with sky-mirror pools. The sweet spot in between, where acidic peat and calcium-rich sand mingle, is a fertile grassland; the machair. It reaches as far as the wind can blow sand.

In the last chapter I discovered a community of people benefiting from peatland and working to protect it, but machair is a habitat that is actually created by a community. I'm booked into a campsite next to the Balranald reserve, which is managed by crofters in collaboration with the Royal Society for the Protection of Birds (RSPB). As I park up and open the door, snatches of sound blow past: singing skylarks and the rasping call of a corncrake.

I walk along the coast to see the machair for myself, and it's mind-glowingly beautiful. Traditionally each family has an allocation of croft land to grow food and raise livestock. The land is marked out into strips which are cultivated in rotation. Half the strips lie fallow and are covered with wild flowers. Each strip has a different history, and so each has a different community of flowers. Some are strewn with tiny wild pansies, yellow and mauve, while others are thick with orchids, lady's bedstraw, harebells and kidney vetch. Other strips are growing a mix of oats, bere barley and rye from traditional seed. Weeds like poppies, fumitory and charlock seem to be tolerated. These crops are used to feed the cows through the winter. This landscape is the total opposite of a peatland. If you laid down on a bog, at best you'd end up soaking wet, and at worst you'd disappear into the mire to be preserved as a bog-body. Here it's a joy to lie on the well-draining sandy soil.

I spot a large bumblebee stumbling between the plant stems. Its bulky body, covered in thick hairs, means it can survive in this colder climate, but it appears to be exhausted. I lie down next to it and offer it different flowers. Red clover is accepted enthusiastically. It extends its proboscis and methodically works through all the flowers of the cluster, probing to the bottom of each for an energy-boost of nectar. When I hold out bird's foot trefoil it embraces the flower and plunges its whole head between the voluptuous petals to guzzle like a baby. Eventually it has enough energy to rev up its wings and take off, flying to a rabbit burrow in a sandbank where its nest must be.

Intensive farming in the rest of the UK means that now this particular species, the great yellow bumblebee, is only found at the far edges of the country in these flower-rich meadows. With my nose down at soil level I can see a whole community of creeping beasties crawling between the grass blades. The plants feed them and they in turn feed the birds that nest here. I watch a lapwing searching for insects to feed its chicks. A crop of oats ripples in the breeze, and sand martins swoop low to pick off flying bugs before they are blown away.

This sheltered grassy world, just a few feet high, is the domain of the corncrake. Here they are hidden from predators like gulls. If the vegetation becomes too dense, they can't move about in it, so a meadow that is cut at the end of each summer is perfect. Once found in flower-rich hay meadows all over Europe, this bird has declined catastrophically in the last 40 years, but on North Uist its rhythmic rasping call is still the sound of summer. I sit quietly drawing the landscape. The craking sound moves around the field, sometimes within feet of me, but still the bird remains invisible. Sometimes I can hear a more intimate cooing when the male is communicating with its partner, but only once does it break cover and I get a momentary glimpse. This sheltered life is in stark contrast to the epic journey it must take to get here. Each spring it must fly 6,000 miles from central Africa to reach these fields where it can raise chicks.

[opposite] *Corncrake and painted lady butterflies*

[following pages] *Sand martins over the corn fields*

One name kept coming up in conversations about the machair. Ena McDonald is in her eighties, and has been involved in crofting for most of her life. A friend agrees to introduce me. As we arrive in her yard, Ena has just finished feeding the hens. Her silver hair is wrapped in a headscarf against the wind. She greets us in Gaelic, but switches to English for me, with a lilting Hebridean accent. In her neat sitting-room, family photos show her with her son, Angus, and grandchildren who now run the farm. However, nobody here sits still for long, as there are always jobs to do. I have volunteered to help weed the vegetable garden, which is sheltered from livestock and wind by a stone wall. It's a pleasant way to chat, working on our hands and knees on the soft ground amongst seedlings of carrots, cauliflower and lettuce. I wonder how the plants grow so well on what looks like sand, and Ena explains how every winter, crofters gather the seaweed washed up by winter storms and spread it on all the fields. It adds important nutrients and also gives body to the soil, to stop the sand and seeds blowing away. 'I used to gather seaweed with a horse and cart, doing all the work by hand with a fork,' she laughs. 'Now my son uses a tractor and spreader. It makes life so much easier.'

She has a good perspective from her many years of working the land, and explains to me how the corncrake used to be much more common. 'It all went wrong for the bird when they started subsidising us to grow crops. You had to put three hundredweight of artificial fertiliser on the field and then use a herbicide to kill the weeds. Luckily I knew the man at the depot, and he didn't force me to buy the weedkiller. My son Angus was in school, but was also earning money spraying for other farmers. One of them offered to let him borrow the tractor to spray our fields. Angus told him, 'If I brought that home, my mother would shoot it!'

When Ena tells me that she used to do her weeding at 5.30 in the morning, I am reminded of the refrain from the last chapter, that the younger generation don't know about hard work. 'I had holidaymakers in the house in summer to make extra money, and I would have to do the gardening before making breakfasts,' she says.

[opposite] *Lapwing on the machair*

But she put her extra money to good use. In Oban one day, with time to spare before the ferry, she visited the livestock market. She bought a Highland cow, and that was the beginning of the now famous and respected Ardbhan Fold.

Ena's hard work continued, and she became chairperson of the Scottish Crofting Federation. She tells me about a photo that caught the attention of her grandson. 'He asked me, "Granny, is that you getting married?"' In fact it was a picture of her with Prince Charles, when in 2006 she went to London to be presented with the MBE for services to crofting.

The mosaic of croft land is so valuable for nesting birds because it provides a varied buffet to choose from. The fallow strips are full of insects and seeds, or if the birds prefer worms, they can visit recently ploughed arable land. Each croft is only big enough to support a few cattle for personal use, so to make crofting viable, the community must work together to share their time and resources. Most crofters also have a full-time paid job to make ends meet, and so must sow crops, harvest them and care for their livestock on evenings and weekends. When you're pushed for time, it's easier and quicker to open a sack of artificial fertiliser instead of collecting winter seaweed. It's safer to harvest a crop early as silage, before it is damaged by the weather or eaten by the geese. Silage is a green crop that is still full of sap and is wrapped in plastic bales to ferment. In the past, crofters waited for the crop to set seed and dry. 'The harvest was weeks of work,' says Ena, 'but the whole community got involved.' Nowadays many young people leave the island for work, so there's a smaller community workforce, and silage has the advantage of being harvested by machine. But silage means fewer wildflowers set seed, and corncrakes can't raise their chicks before the fields are mown. And when there are no more sheaves stacked to dry in the fields in autumn, there is less seed for birds like the corn bunting.

There are always new threats to the landscape, and the latest pressure, quite literally, is from heavier breeds of cattle. Many crofters have started to farm bigger, non-traditional breeds, which put on weight faster. In the same way that enormous

[opposite] *Redshank and cows*

marrows win rosettes at agricultural shows, so larger, more muscular livestock are also successful. There is a great sense of pride in crofting – and it's all about who produces prize-winning animals, not who makes the most profit. Traditionally cattle are kept off the machair fields in the summer months so that winter fodder can be grown. The animals are put inland on the hill-ground to graze, but the new breeds need more food than is available on the hill and so they graze the machair more intensively. They are also less hardy than the Highland cow with its long woolly coat, and in winter they must be kept indoors. This is much easier for the hard-pressed crofter than working in the wind and rain, but the seed-eating birds like twite, linnet and corn bunting are declining without the scavenged grains.

So what is the future of the machair? I speak to Jamie Boyle, who has just retired after 35 years working on Uist for the RSPB. 'Machair is very resilient,' he says. 'It thrives on neglect.' He explains that when inland croft-land is abandoned it only takes a few years before it fills with rushes, but machair remains as a dry grassland. Simply by adding seaweed to the soil and by grazing with livestock, crofters can bring it back into use, and also increase the machair's biodiversity. 'Getting fertiliser onto the islands is incredibly expensive,' says Jamie. This and the price of fuel has discouraged many crofters from intensive farming. But to keep crofting going, agri-environmental subsidies are essential. For crofters to receive these payments, the ploughing in spring must take place before the ground-nesting birds lay their eggs. Grass must not be cut until August, so that the corncrake chicks are old enough to leave the nest and escape the mowers. And the benefits are clear. 'Uist is still a real stronghold for the corncrake,' Jamie tells me, 'the population has been stable for 20 years now.' For many crofters, the rasping call is the normal sound of summer, and they can't see what all the fuss is about. But the fact that so many tourists come here to hear them, means they do bring financial benefit. 'The owner of the Balranald campsite calls the corncrake his business partner,' says Jamie.

To celebrate their rich natural heritage, the Outer Hebrides Wildlife Festival was started in 2022. This community-led festival is run not only for visitors, but for

[opposite] *Hebridean summer, terns*

locals as well, so they can learn more about the fantastic wildlife on their doorstep. In 2024 the programme included courses on nature writing, wildlife photography, snorkelling safaris, boat tours and guided walks. Jamie told me that in the first year of the festival, the RSPB film *Beyond a Tangled Shore* was shown. I used to work in the RSPB Film Unit in the 1990s, and even then, it was one of our older (and most beautiful) films. It was made in the 1970s on North Uist – over 50 years ago. Jamie reminded me of the film's final images: a croft house with a stormy sky gathering behind it. The message was that the threats of depopulation and intensification of farming would lead to an uncertain future. 'It made us laugh,' he says, 'because that's exactly what we're still talking about, 50 years later.'

Before I leave North Uist, I want to get up close and personal with the machair one last time. The added bonus of lying down in the short grass means you are out of the wind. I watch a redshank standing atop a fence post, gripping tight and balancing into each gust. The lapwing chicks are settling down for the night. The adult fluffs out its belly feathers and the youngsters push underneath for warmth and shelter. By 11pm the sun is dipping to the sea horizon and, in the warm glowing light, a short-eared owl glides across a field of pink ragged robin. The flowers dance gently as the breeze drops and the skylarks seize the chance to sing in the evening calm.

The way our landscape looks and operates is hugely influenced by how it is grazed, whether by domesticated animals, or wild animals like deer. I want to investigate this further, and I decide to visit the island of Islay, which is grazed both by farmed livestock and wild geese. I want to find out about the conflict between these two, and also to see if there is any solution to this new problem of heavier breeds of cattle on the west coast.

[opposite] *Short-eared owl*

ISLAY

CHAPTER FOUR

FARMLAND

On much of the west coast, the pounding Atlantic waves blast out a rocky shore. Shallow estuaries are rare. Sea lochs are mostly steep-sided glacier-gouged fjords, but on Islay, geology has created something different. Part of the faultline that forms the Great Glen (bisecting Scotland between Inverness and Fort William, and containing Loch Ness) continues south-west and cuts Islay almost in two, creating two shallow sea lochs. Birds, migrating in autumn from their breeding grounds in the high Arctic to winter further south, head for these important mud-flats and salt marshes to refuel after their long sea-crossing. The south-facing Loch Indaal has a small tidal range influenced by the Irish Sea, but only a few miles away the Atlantic-facing Loch Gruinart has a tidal range of 3.5 metres. Twice a day the mud-flats are exposed and thousands of wading birds feed on worms and other invertebrates.

In November the days are short and nights are longer. Arriving on Islay with the mid-afternoon ferry, Mark and I drive straight to Loch Gruinart. It's low tide and there's so much activity. Birds are congregating on the sky-mirror channels and dark mud-banks, not in well-spaced feeding groups, but gathered into tighter communities of different species in anticipation of dusk. A patina of feathered shapes and contact calls is superimposed on the rippled texture of sandbanks and sea. Bold zigzags of flying oystercatchers cut across the sinuous tidal channels. Leggy long-billed curlews stalk past the rounded bodies of preening wigeon. Shelduck sift the shallow water, their curved cummerbunds reflecting underneath them in reverse. With shrill alarm, tight flocks of tiny dunlin take flight, spooking the larger peewits which lift off with slow beats of rounded wings. The distant yapping of barnacle geese suddenly escalates, and a huge white-noise flock rises from fields behind us. Speckled black and white, the flock crescendos, resolving as it passes low over our heads into skeins of cackling goose-shaped silhouettes. They glide down to roost on the mud. Although there are no foxes or badgers on the island, they feel safer sleeping in an open area. Unlike the other birds, geese don't actually feed in the estuary, as they are grass eaters. The Gulf Stream keeps the island climate mild, and grass grows on Islay throughout the winter. Seventy

Brown hares

per cent of all the barnacle geese from Greenland use the island as a winter-feeding ground – almost 30,000 birds. Forty per cent of Greenland's white-fronted geese also live here in the winter months.

Next morning the tide is up, a flat sheen with only a few mallard disturbing the cloud reflections. I'm on my way to talk to James How, the senior site manager of the Royal Society for the Protection of Birds' Islay reserves. The RSPB has a farm at Loch Gruinart. Farmland is not a wild habitat any more than a garden is. Both are landscapes artificially modified by humans, but both can be valuable for wildlife.

James and I look down over the green fields at the head of the loch, which are covered in grazing geese and cattle, and he tells me about reserve's history. In the 1830s a seawall was built to reclaim the salt-marsh and turn it into farmland. In 1984 the RSPB bought the land around Loch Gruinart. Until that time sports shooting was big business for the Islay estates, and numbers of barnacle geese had declined to about 6,000. At the beginning, the reserve was all about producing enough grass to sustain the geese through the winter. The meadows were rented out to farmers for grazing in summer, but no-one wanted to rent the rough hill-ground, so eventually the RSPB decided to farm it all.

James comes from a nature conservation background, but studied at agricultural college. When he took on the job he found himself between the two conflicting island communities, of conservationists and farmers. With the aid of modern fertilisers and herbicides, Islay farmers had become skilled at producing immaculate fields of lush grass to feed their prize-winning herds of cattle. But the grass was also perfect food for the overwintering geese, and their numbers increased. Huge flocks were compacting the fields and impacting profits. Substantial subsidies have been introduced to compensate the farmers, but tensions continue.

James' job is to show how good farming can produce food for both humans and wildlife, and it's not just the geese that he's farming for. By the 1990s, conservationists started to realise that many other farmland birds were in danger of disappearing, and nowadays summer visitors, like corncrakes and nesting waders, are all catered for in the RSPB's land management plan. 'My job is to deliver the best range of habitats,' James explains, 'and some of the main tools to achieve this are the grazing animals.' He is constantly innovating to find new, sustainable ways to farm.

A recent innovation is rotational grazing. Rather than letting the cattle range over the whole field, the animals are fenced into smaller areas that they graze hard for a few days, before being moved to the next area. 'It's actually more like the farming of the past, when fields were much smaller,' James explains. 'The grass is able to grow longer in between being grazed, and so it can make more energy. It sends the excess down to its roots for storage. This reduces our use of fertiliser by two-thirds.' Having a big organisation behind them means that they can afford to experiment, but the farm must make a profit. 'Each animal is an expensive piece of grazing equipment,' says James, 'so they must pay their own way.'

Sheep are used to nibble down the dock and ragwort plants left by the geese, but the RSPB has decided to reduce the number that they farm. Since the Clearances in the 1800s, sheep have been put onto rough, west coast ground, but James points out that they are really Mediterranean animals. In Scotland it costs £20 a year to keep each one healthy in the wet climate, treating them for fluke, worms, scab, fly strike etc. All these treatments are bad for the environment, as well as the farm's budget.

James introduces me to Eion Brown, the RSPB's Islay Farms Manager. Eion was born on the island and speaks some Gaelic, but that's not why I struggle to understand him. He comes from a farming background and his conversation is full of terms like 'frame score' and 'EBV'. I have to keep asking him to translate (EBV means Estimated Breeding Value). Eion takes me to a farmyard where a group of small heifers are feeding from a trailer. 'This lot are real liquorice allsorts,' he says. 'They're from a Belgian blue cross Limousin bull on a white shorthorn cross Highland cow and they're in calf to our native Angus bull.' He laughs as I scribble in my notebook. 'Folk think farmers spend their day standing around chewing on a straw, but farming's a complicated business.' He gives me a handful of the food from the trailer, and despite the day being cold, it's warm! This is a staple of cattle-farming on Islay. It's silage mixed with draff, the mashed fermented barley from one of the many whisky distilleries on the island. 'It's a pleasant job to fork this out in winter, as it warms up your feet inside your boots,' he says.

We go to see a group of Aberdeen Angus bulls in their field. They're huge and muscular, and all are glossy black with bronze rings in their noses. When Eion starts to name the animals, I have the same feeling as when my son talks about different makes of car. To my untrained eye they all look the same. 'That's Joey Essex and there's Johnny English. They're both large American-style bulls.' He explains that Angus bulls are named using the initials of their mother (in this case Jessica Erica). All this seems a long way from growing grass for geese, but Eion is responsible for making the farm run efficiently. He's been trying to solve the problem of why the cows are producing fewer calves.

'I've farmed on Islay for 22 years, but I've learned more in the last three years than in the previous 19,' Eion says. On Islay, as on the machair of North Uist, cattle are being bred to a bigger size. Supermarkets want standard cuts of meat to fit their packaging and their pricing, and so if all the animals conform to the same size, farmers get a better price. But unless he supplements their feed, which is expensive, his hill-grazed animals won't get enough nutrition to produce the bigger calves, and so birth-rates are dropping. And bigger calves give another problem. On intensive farms, cows regularly have caesareans, but they can only have three or four and then their breeding days are finished. Intensively reared cattle are kept indoors a lot of the time, but the cattle on Islay need to be outside doing their important job of grazing. One day, after a particularly difficult calving, Eion decided to look online for cattle breeds that produced smaller offspring. He found an old-fashioned pure-bred Aberdeen Angus bull for sale. This breed, originally from the north-east of Scotland, had nearly disappeared with the fashion for bigger animals. 'Buying that bull was the best thing we ever did,' said Eion. His smaller calves can still just grow to supermarket size when sent away for fattening up, but are better suited to the food available and their wiry coat withstands the Scottish weather.

I go for a walk to the mouth of Loch Gruinart, where tall sand dunes are piled up by the Atlantic breakers. They're stabilised by marram grass, and farmers have used this ground for centuries to provide shelter for their cattle in winter. The sand is free-draining, so the ground isn't muddy and poached up around the feed troughs. I can hear the cries of red-billed choughs, but it takes me a while to track them down. Even though they are pecking vigorously through dried cow pats, searching for dung-beetle maggots, they still look elegant with their glossy black

plumage and scarlet legs and beaks. There are only 30 to 40 pairs of this charismatic bird left on Islay. RSPB has been working with farmers to stabilise their population.

One of the problems affecting them is the veterinary medicine that's used to treat cows for intestinal worms. The chemicals kill insects in the cow's gut, but also persist in the dung on the ground. The waste-disposal insects that process the dung are also poisoned – meaning no food for the chough. Normally all cows are dosed regularly, but the RSPB has been working in collaboration with Islay vets to speed up screening for worm eggs. Normally samples would take several days to be processed in a lab, but the new 'Fecpak' (Feacal Egg Count Pack) can be used on-site. The vets can count how many worm eggs are in the sample, to identify cows that don't need to be treated. Everyone is happy, as the farmers spend less money on medicines, the drug companies reduce problems with drug-resistance, and there are more dung-beetle larvae for the chough.

The cows create habitat for other rare animals in the sand-dunes – specifically, two insects that I've never even heard of before, the northern colletes mining bee and the short-necked oil beetle. These insects rely on the overwintering cattle to keep the vegetation grazed low so they can continue their extraordinary relationship. The newly hatched oil beetle larva (called a triungulin) climbs to the top of a flower and waits for a mining bee to visit and feed. It jumps onto the bee and holds on using special hooks. Once transported to the bee's burrow in the dunes, it spends the winter fattening up on food stores gathered by the bee, and emerges as an adult beetle the following spring to continue the life cycle.

After a cold morning outdoors I'm glad when James invites me for lunch at his house. His kitchen overlooks fields sloping down to the loch, and he tells me that he can read goose rings from the garden. To humans, all barnacle geese look pretty identical, so to study them, scientists place plastic rings with a large three-digit code on their legs.

Each winter about 150 birds are caught and ringed, using cannon nets. This is a technique I know about, as I spent a lot of a weekends as a teenager helping my

[opposite] *Choughs*

Dad cannon-net gulls. An area in front of the net is baited with grain to encourage the birds to feed in a concentrated area. The front of the net is attached to projectiles which are fired into the air above the birds, pulling the net over them before they can take flight. I remember that during the time of the IRA bombings in the 1980s, my Dad got better at driving within the speed limit. He didn't want to be stopped by the police and have to explain why he had gunpowder and detonators in the car! Cannon netting can be hours of boredom, waiting for the birds to land in the right place, followed by excitement as the net fires and you run to see what you have caught.

Goose-ringing has provided lots of fascinating information. Barnacle geese live on average about 14 years, but the oldest recorded age is 27 years. They live in family groups, and an adult pair will stay together winter and summer. There are two populations in the UK. Those that breed on Svalbard, to the north-east, winter in the Solway Firth, and those that breed in Greenland, to the north-west, winter on Islay. The two populations don't mix much at all.

James tells me about his favourite goose, with leg ring ULB. 'He's the same age as my daughter. We know he's a male from his head measurement when he was ringed. When I go out with a bucket of grain he recognises me and brings his family group over to feed. He's been arriving every autumn in the field by my house for over 20 years, and he's never been recorded off the reserve. Maybe that's why he's survived so long.' Ringing has shown that birds which habitually graze on the reserve have fewer shotgun pellets in their bodies. But why are geese being shot at?

Geese have wintered on Islay for thousands of years, feeding on the salt marshes. The maritime climate means that grass grows throughout the year – great for farmers and geese alike. The government pays farmers many thousands of pounds in compensation, but after pressure from farmers it has also begun funding a cull. James disagrees with the way this cull is being done. Multi-action shotguns are used, which allow the marksman to carry on shooting as the birds go out of range. Because the shot scatters, the further away the target, the more geese will receive

[opposite] *Barnacle geese*

injuries. Beyond 40 metres there is 40 per cent more chance of injuring other birds. After 1,000 shots, 400 birds will have a non-lethal injury. On the reserve the geese know they are safe from humans, and they will stay grazing next to the road, giving good views for tourists.

In recent years farmers have had a new ally to help regulate goose numbers. In 2010 sea eagles started breeding on Islay and on neighbouring Jura. In summer the eagles eat hares or rabbits, and scavenge on deer and seal carcasses. In autumn and winter, there is a constant buffet of geese on offer. They mainly seem to be taking the weak or injured geese, but as the flock takes flight every time an eagle appears, feeding is disrupted, which benefits the farmers. 'There were 17 sea eagles last year,' says James. 'They seemed to operate as a group, the older ones throwing goose carcasses for younger ones to practise catching in mid-air.' This more natural way of controlling numbers has the added benefit of encouraging natural history tourism at an otherwise quiet time of year. It's a wonderful spectacle when thousands of geese fill the sky, jinking and diving away from a swooping eagle.

The 2022–3 Avian Flu outbreak had an even bigger effect, with an estimated 5,000 geese dying on Islay. 'A flock of 50 ravens gathered here,' says James. 'I imagine it looked similar on the battlegrounds of the Jacobite rebellion. In the spring we collected a thousand goose skeletons from the silage fields.'

Having learned so much from James and Eion, I decide to return to Islay in August for the main event of the farming year – The Islay, Jura and Colonsay Agricultural Show (the 176th!). I book my van on the ferry, but online there is no information that I can find about where or what time it takes place. Of course everyone on the island already knows, and it's not an event run for outsiders. I spot a few signs with the date and 'CASH ONLY' in big letters, and asking around, I'm directed up a narrow track to a wide field where pens have been assembled to create judging rings. From the rows of parked cars I'm greeted by the sound of cattle bellowing, kids laughing and the smell of burgers frying. Flags flap in the wind above a collection of marquees and a row of vintage tractors, and a generator is powering a bouncy

[opposite] *Snipe*

castle. A loudspeaker keeps up a running commentary of the livestock winners in each category. All of Islay seems to be here. Young couples push children in buggies or queue at the food stalls, and groups of lads are gathering outside the beer tent. The show gives everyone a welcome holiday, as farming can be a solitary business. It's a chance to be proud of what's been achieved. Farming families cluster around their prize animals, polishing hooves and brushing out forelocks. Many of the sheep have their fleeces dyed orange for the show ring, and I spot a few teenagers who have applied the dye to each other too. There's a gymkhana, a dog show, a sheep-shearing demonstration and Highland dancing, but the main event is the sheep and beef judging. I spot Eion in the crowd and he's beaming. His cattle have won in their category.

The show is also an opportunity for learning. I visit James on the RSPB stand, and he tells me about new technology which will soon mean farmers won't have to keep moving fences. Satellite collars can be programmed each day by a mobile phone to contain the cows in a fixed area. The cows are played music when they are approaching the grazing boundary, and learn how to stay within their virtual field. 'Historically farmers have been really good at working out how to produce food more efficiently,' James tells me. 'Now there's a new challenge, and younger farmers are having to find ways to farm more sustainably. But the agricultural community are used to coming up with solutions – it's what they do every day.'

In the show-ring, calves and young heifers are being led around, often by younger members of the family. There are constant battles of will between a reluctant animal and a young person much lighter than them. These young farmers are impressively determined, and will not give up despite being pushed around. It's a quality that every farmer needs. I walk past a pick-up truck with a sticker on the back window: 'Screw a farmer – everyone else does.' This way of life is at the mercy of many factors outside the farmer's control, like the weather and government decisions. And now there's a new threat to their livelihood.

[opposite] *Islay, Jura and Colonsay Agricultural Show*

Lapwings in the stubble field

Potentially valuable subsidies for increasing carbon sequestration have led to tenant farms being taken back in hand by estates for rewilding. Because a large part of Scotland is owned by a few big landowners, changes in land management can have widespread results. 'Rewilding is one form of land management, but not suitable everywhere,' says James. 'It's unhelpfully opened up yet another polarised view between farmers and conservationists. Eating meat has had bad press recently, but farming livestock provides biodiversity. Eating meat from nature-friendly farms is positive.'

On Islay, two very different communities with different skills, priorities, and even languages, have had to come together to solve the problem of how to use land sustainably for the future of both humans and wildlife. 'If you do the job well,' James tells me, 'farmers will accept all sorts of different opinions.' He's been helped by the island mentality. 'You have to get along. Of course farmers fall out, but they know that in an island community, they can't let it get out of hand. It's newcomers who don't always understand that, and sometimes end up leaving.' The community spirit is perfectly demonstrated by the 'Islay Wave'. It always catches me out when I first arrive, and I can't believe it still continues, especially on such a big island. On Islay all car drivers wave at any other car that they pass on the road, whether they know them or not. Here, everyone is welcomed into the community while they are on the island.

On Islay, grazing animals are vital for maintaining the grassland habitat, but in other parts of Scotland, too many grazers can destroy a landscape. I want to find out how native deer, and also people, affect the Scottish Highlands, so I decide to head up the coast towards Fort William.

LOCH ARKAIG

CHAPTER FIVE

WOODLAND

An ancient Caledonian pine stands high on the hill above Loch Arkaig. The growth-rings in its gnarled limbs contain the history of three centuries of west coast wind, rain and sun. The land is mostly too steep and rocky for growing crops, and trees have found a foothold here for 10,000 years. Shade-loving plants, fungi and insects have had time to build a complex community – a Celtic rainforest.

This 'granny pine' has somehow survived, but over the years many other pines have succumbed to a succession of land-management decisions. Her parents would have been growing here in 1611, when surveyors for the Crown came looking for shipbuilding timber. They reported finding trees of impressive height and girth, to provide masts for sailing ships. At that time wolves still roamed these forests. In 1745 the trees provided shelter for Bonnie Prince Charlie when he took refuge after defeat at the battle of Culloden. Our granny's roots may be entwined around the fabled hoard of gold coins sent to support the Jacobite rebellion.

In Victorian times our tree was in her prime, but this was when stalking became popular. Every year her offspring were grazed out by high deer numbers. In 1942 Loch Arkaig was a training ground for commandos en route to World War Two. A fire which started during exercises swept through the forest, killing many of her siblings, and blackened stumps still dot the hillside to this day. In the 1960s pine plantations were popular. The Achnacarry Estate sold two blocks of land to the Forestry Commission. The land was ploughed to drain it, and non-native lodgepole pine and Sitka spruce were planted around the remnant native trees. Many were gradually shaded out and died on their feet, remaining today as bleached skeletons.

By the early twenty-first century, commercial plantations were no longer being harvested by horses but by huge machines. Roads would have had to be built to reach this plantation and that would have cost more than the value of the trees. The two blocks of land were put up for sale and the local community decided to buy them under the National Forest Land Scheme. To fund the purchase they approached the Woodland Trust, who ran a campaign to raise money from their members. One thousand hectares are now owned and managed by the Arkaig Community Forest (ACF), and the Woodland Trust.

A thousand hectares is a huge swathe of hillside, although it's a tiny portion of the surrounding Achnacarry Estate, which is 28 times that size. But as Henry Dobson, estate manager for the Woodland Trust, explained to me, it's enough to provide an example of what's possible. Over the last 500 years this land has been owned either by the Camerons of Lochiel, or at times was forfeited by the Crown, but it has always had one owner and has always been subject to the land-use model of the day, whether timber-felling, sheep grazing, deer-stalking or even training for war. 'Now, having the community intrinsically engaged in the landscape gives much more resilience,' says Henry. 'You can't have one individual changing the land use overnight.' Henry introduced me to many of the local people working in the landscape, but first he showed me around the forest. We spent five hours together, and I was scribbling notes almost the whole time, such was Henry's enthusiasm, knowledge and generosity.

When he got the job, Henry's first task was to work out how to extract the non-native pines. In areas that already had road access, modern machines could be used, but the area called the Gusach (meaning pine forest in Gaelic) was extremely remote. Rather than build an expensive road which would damage the habitat, he commissioned a company to build and operate a barge to bring the logs across the loch to the road on the north shore. The barge, called *Each-Uisge*, the water-horse, had to be transported there in sections, to fit between two veteran oak trees forming the narrowest point on the road. Timber is driven onto the barge on a truck called a forwarder. This runs on biofuel, not only to reduce fossil-fuel consumption, but so that any fuel spillage will not contaminate the loch. Henry combined these innovative modern solutions with the traditional way of bringing the logs down off the hill, and employed Tarzan, a Comtois logging horse, and his owner, Simon Dakin. The sale of the timber pays for its removal.

To start with, the hillside is left covered in tree stumps, but this dead wood provides food for invertebrates which start to break it down. 'In a healthy woodland you should have one-third living trees, one-third standing dead trees and one-third lying timber,' Henry tells me. The rotting wood will return nutrients to the soil for the regenerating native trees. In order for these young, tender trees to get a start, deer numbers must be reduced, as they find the new growth irresistible.

The original plantation fencing had fallen into disrepair. This was mended and stalkers employed to reduce deer numbers inside it. And now as we walk through the felled land we can already see the results. The commercial trees were planted close together, which forced them to race each other for the light above, growing straight and tall. This excluded all light from the forest floor. Now seeds that have lain in the soil for 60 years feel the warmth of the sun, and can germinate. Foxgloves and lady's bedstraw are flowering, and the leaves of silver birch trees shimmer in the breeze. Steep ravines, that were inaccessible for planting commercial pines, provided mini 'arks' where native trees could survive: holly, oak, willow, rowan and alder. Henry pointed out rowan seedlings growing under a broad oak. Birds roosting in the branches had been eating rowan berries elsewhere and had defecated the seeds. The woodland is slowly reverting from a monoculture back to a community of extraordinary complexity.

This complexity occurs at all levels. At a landscape level, different trees grow in the ground that best suits them. Caledonian pines prefer well-draining slopes, whereas alder is happy when its roots are waterlogged. This variety provides living spaces, or niches, for different animals. For example, the chequered skipper butterfly, which in Scotland is only found within a 25-mile radius of Fort William, needs sunny, but damp, sheltered glades. As the forest returns, so does the butterfly.

Individual trees can themselves provide a plethora of niches. Compared to the straight trunks of the plantation trees, the gnarled and twisted branches of oaks with their nooks and crannies are communities in their own right. The caterpillars that feed on the leaves sustain the great tits that nest in the branches, which are in turn eaten by tawny owls breeding in holes in the trunk. And even once it's toppled, an oak provides many more decades of shelter. Beetles burrowing under the bark feed woodpeckers which chisel out a nest-hole in the dead branches. The upturned root plate provides dryer micro-niches where other trees can germinate above the browsing level of deer. And then of course there are the fungi, about which we are still learning so much. Not only do they decompose the dead wood, but mycorrhizal fungi connect tree roots underground and help distribute nutrients between trees, allowing the woodland to act as a community rather than a group of individuals.

Fungi also create communities above ground, when they grow structures to shelter other organisms. On the tree bark here, alongside mosses, liverworts and ferns, are many different lichens. These are a collaboration between a fungus and algae. The fungus provides the main structure – tufted, lobbed or encrusting. It doesn't have roots, but anchors itself to the tree and traps water from the rain. It gives shelter to green algae, or sometimes a photosynthesising bacteria, which can convert the sun's rays into carbohydrates which it shares with the fungus for growth and energy. The algae give colour to the lichen – a whole spectrum of different greens.

Henry offers to show me one of the lichen celebrities of Loch Arkaig: 'It's the one that all the lichen experts get really excited about.' I follow as he leaves the path and plunges downhill through waist-high bracken. We eventually reach an ancient hazel tree that is leaning out over a fast-flowing burn. Hopping between rocks in the stream, he points out a dark spotted lichen, the Norwegian specklebelly. This lichen also contains a third partner, a cyanobacteria which can fix nitrogen from the air. The specklebelly prefers the bark of hazel, as it is less acidic than other trees. But deer also find hazel very desirable and this tree has probably only survived because of its inaccessible location. 'This lichen only occurs in Arkaig Forest on two hazel trees,' Henry tells me. And this has given him a dilemma. Ideally the ACF would like regeneration to happen naturally. However, if disaster befell the hazel tree, its whole residential community would also be lost.

This prompted me to question why something that is rare is any more valuable than something that is common. Should we not celebrate the lichens that have managed to thrive in the reduced circumstances of our modern world? There are other woodland inhabitants that have also become rare because of humans. Wild cats, golden eagles, red squirrels and capercaillies all need large landscapes. 'Typically, it's the specialist life forms that have struggled to survive,' says Henry. But he explains that diversity makes the forest more resilient. 'These are the ones we need to spread back out for the influence they have on the wider forest community as it recovers.' For example, a variety of plant species will encourage diversity in the animal population; if blaeberry increases with reduced grazing, it will provide food for capercaillies.

[opposite] *Great tits*

Global warming will put extra pressures on the forest, so to speed up regeneration, ACF have set up a tree nursery. This also provides two part-time local jobs. I speak to the manager Anna Macfie, who allows me to visit the polytunnel where she works. The main threats to her tree seedlings are the many plant diseases that could attack them, so all visitors must go through biosecurity. At the gate I brush all mud off my boots, wash the soles and walk across a disinfectant mat.

The polytunnel has the atmosphere of a well-run orphanage. There are thousands of baby trees each growing in their individual cells. On a whiteboard are written 'medical notes' – instructions on which plants to check for disease and how to water different seedlings. An incubator stands in the corner for particularly delicate plants. Anna has been experimenting with different compost to see what best promotes germination and growth. There are so many variables, and she makes notes to keep track of the successes. To promote germination the pine seeds must be chilled to 2°C for a whole month (this could be what controls the southern limit of the trees). But once sprouted, the seedlings grow faster when it's warm. 'The polytunnel extends the growing season,' she tells me. 'The warmth allows the pine seedlings to grow 10cm between the spring equinox and mid-May.' Later they will be put outside to get used to the Scottish climate. In 18 months they will grow into 25cm-long green bottle-brushes that are ready for planting out.

ACF, with help from the Woodland Trust's Volunteer Seed Collection Project, organises community seed-collecting days in Arkaig Forest for broadleaf trees. Pine cones are collected by a tree-climbing team in winter. The pines have spent thousands of years adapting to conditions on that particular hillside and have built-in genetic variety to respond to changing conditions. For example, some Caledonian pines produce phenolic compounds to deter insect pests. These chemicals give pine their characteristic smell, but they are metabolically expensive to produce. Some individual trees don't bother going to the trouble, but allow aphids to live on their leaves. This attracts wood ants which farm the aphids, and at the same time eat any other insects on the tree. This strategy is successful only as long as there are wood ants living nearby. The seed-collection team must therefore collect from different trees to ensure this genetic adaptability continues.

[opposite] *Fieldfares*

In the polytunnel I meet volunteer Charlie, an ICU nurse who is recovering from long-Covid. He is doing a horticulture course and gaining work experience with ACF. He is transplanting one-month-old pines into individual cells where they will have more space to grow. 'It's amazing to think that these tiny seedlings could be huge pine trees one day.' He explains to me that concentrating on this positive task has really helped him get through his illness.

All around us is new growth. Hazel seedlings are packed in to that staple of west-coast gardening, the beachcombed fish-box. I can also see alder, hawthorn, downy birch and wych elm. The wavy-edged leaves of oaks spread wide to catch the sun's rays, and thousands of transplanted pine seedlings reach for the light, their wispy leaves like small green hands. Seeing these two species next to each other I marvel at such different approaches to the conversion of sunlight and carbon dioxide into wood. The flat blades of the evergreen oaks are much more efficient for half the year. But when temperatures plummet in autumn the soft fleshy leaves shrivel and fall to the ground. All the energy used to produce those leaves is thrown away. The trees must wait for fungi and soil bacteria to break down the leaves and release the carbon back into the air. The tougher pine needles can carry on working throughout the seasons and for many years.

The rarest trees in the nursery are the aspens. It's not a tree that I've seen before, so Charlie has to point them out. I'm used to identifying birds by the way that they move and sound, but Charlie shows me how this also applies to aspens. Their heart-shaped leaves flutter in the breeze, making a constant noise of gentle clapping. Aspens are less rare in Norway, where more people shoot deer for food, and sheep-farming isn't subsidised like here. In Scotland they've been grazed almost to extinction and only survive on remote cliff-faces. They have two strategies for reproduction. Some produce flowers and seeds, but here on the west coast all of their young are regularly eaten. Those that reproduce by growing suckers still persist, and two of these natural clones still grow in the forest. Anna hopes to obtain cuttings from flowering aspens in nearby glens and graft them onto root stock from the suckering aspen. She will need at least 20 of these surrogate mothers to maintain genetic diversity in the forest.

Great spotted woodpecker

Driving around the local area, I am surprised at how even small gardens have 2-metre-high deer fences around them. Because Achnacarry is a stalking estate, it traditionally has encouraged high numbers of deer for sport. This has created the open, denuded landscape of Scotland where the forest can't regrow. ACF have committed to reducing deer to numbers that will allow vegetation to return, typically two to seven deer per square kilometre. I go to meet Rob Coope who is managing the deer larder, which takes the venison. The facilities are luxurious compared to anything I'm used to. Here the cold store is separate from the processing area, so you don't get freezing cold when working.

Rob has worked in forestry for many years and explains why culling leads to better health for the deer. 'High densities of deer mean there is less food, which leads to smaller deer, low reproduction rates and high winter mortality. They've nowhere to shelter from the weather as they've eaten all the cover.' Deer are an important part of the woodland ecosystem, but with no natural predators like wolves, it is down to humans to keep their numbers low enough that new trees can grow. ACF pays local stalkers for any deer they shoot in the woodland. Their skills are appreciated and this cooperation with people from the wider landscape is beneficial. Most of the animals are red deer, although sika deer, introduced from east Asia, are becoming more common as they are more likely to hide in thick undergrowth like invasive rhododendron or pine plantation, and emerge to graze at night. They can interbreed with the native red deer, which is a serious threat to their genetic future.

Local people are taking deer management qualifications which includes learning to shoot deer and veterinary training. Butchering and selling the venison not only provides jobs, but provides a connection to the woodland for people in the area. People who buy the meat want to learn more about where it comes from and engage with the project. ACF and the Woodland Trust attend deer management meetings with their neighbours. 'In the early days of deer management, the usual way of respecting your neighbour meant putting up a fence so you could do your own thing on each side of it,' Rob tells me. But now the regeneration of the forest is providing inspiration and the estate have committed to reduce deer from

[opposite] *Red deer*

17 to 10 per square kilometre on their own land. Once the forest is re-established, grazing by deer will be vital to maintain variety in the vegetation.

Caledonian pine trees provide the perfect nest-site for ospreys. The lack of lower branches makes it difficult for predators to climb the long trunk, and the open canopy makes it easy to fly in and land. Ospreys became extinct in the UK in the early twentieth century because of egg-collecting and shooting. They eat salmon and trout, so were not popular on sporting estates. They found their way back to Scotland to breed in the 1950s, and although they were still persecuted, there was huge public support for the birds. They were protected by conservation groups until they had re-established themselves. Building artificial nest platforms helped the new birds to breed successfully, and now there are about 250 pairs nesting in the UK, most of them in Scotland where they can find tall trees and a plentiful supply of fish.

In 2017 the Woodland Trust built an artificial nest and installed a live nest-cam in Loch Arkaig Forest – an ambitious task. All the equipment, including solar panels to power the camera, had to be carried into the mountains. This was done before the birds arrived, when there was still winter snow on the ground. Qualified climbers fixed the camera above an artificial nesting platform. The signal had to be bounced two kilometres across the loch to a locally-run broadband service, which sent it out to the wider world. It was a nervous wait to see if birds would nest in front of the camera. A male arrived in early April and was dubbed Lonesome Louis by the watchers, as he waited for a mate. After three weeks the first part of his name could be dropped as a female arrived, later named Aila. People from all over the world joined the osprey-watching community to follow the family throughout the breeding season.

The Woodland Trust have a team of citizen scientists who monitor the camera and log interesting behaviour. One of these is Liz Bracken, who lives above Loch Arkaig and can see the osprey nest across the water from her house. I paid her a visit to find out more. She is a retired nurse with no particular background in ornithology, but she has become an osprey enthusiast. If watchers see the birds

[opposite] *Osprey and chick*

sounding the alarm on camera, they alert Liz and she can check the wider area with a telescope. It might be a golden eagle, or another osprey which has intruded into their territory.

Liz learned a huge amount in those first few years. 'It was fascinating seeing them work things out as an inexperienced couple,' she told me. The first year they laid three eggs but only fledged one chick. In 2018 they again laid three eggs, but these were eaten by a pine marten. The tree has a slippery collar, but a storm-broken branch hung down and allowed the pine marten to bypass this. 'The female didn't know what to do and got up off the eggs. We could only watch it all happen on camera,' says Liz.

In 2021 Aila failed to return from her winter migration to West Africa. Louis paired with a new female and moved to a different site. The first camera had been so popular that the Woodland Trust team set up a new one the following winter. This female was particularly dark and was called Dorcha (Dark) from the Gaelic. Females are distinguished by a dark necklace pattern, and as with all birds of prey, are larger than their mates. She does most of the incubation, as her size makes her best suited to defending her chicks against predators like ravens, owls or other ospreys. Right from the beginning of courtship it is the male who brings food, as he needs to prove he is a good hunter and can catch enough to feed both her and the chicks. He plunge-dives on his prey, and grips the slippery fish tight with his scaly feet. Once airborne, he lines up the fish to point forwards to create the least wind-resistance. The fish brought to the nest are identified via the camera by a rota of citizen scientist volunteers. Louis can bring in up to six fish a day (his all-time record is nine), and more than 500 in a season. They are mostly brown trout, but flat fish, salmon and mackerel also feature on the menu.

The chicks have a pecking order, but Dorcha seems to feed them each in turn. It's fascinating to watch the way she walks around the tiny chicks with her talons curled, to avoid hurting them. She's less careful when bringing new branches to build up the nest, and the youngsters get smacked around the head in a painful comedy routine. Each year the chicks are named through a public vote, and there is a list of all the names on the Woodland Trust website. In 2019 one was named Rannoch to honour Liz, as this is Gaelic for Bracken.

Liz likes to research any questions asked online. 'I'm curious and love to learn things, so I end up posting links to articles on how the chick's feathers grow, or how they digest fishbones.' She has learned so much from hours of watching the birds' body language and listening to calls. 'They have relaxed contact calls, begging calls, and the female even has a call that she only uses when hoodie crows are mobbing her – it's a bit like a quacking duck!' The crows work as a team, trying to steal food that the male has brought.

By welcoming digital visitors to watch ospreys through their website, the Woodland Trust have found the perfect solution to Loch Arkaig's remote location. When people do visit in person, it is often to share or gain knowledge. The forest has become a flagship example of how to restore an ancient woodland. Liz tells me how she joined a seed-collecting visit by the Royal Botanic Garden Edinburgh (RBGE) who came to look for a plant called small cow-wheat. They called it the Goldilocks plant, as it's golden in colour and very fussy. It grows in humid, shady woodlands in a symbiotic relationship with wood ants. Its seed has a heavy carbohydrate part which provides food. The ants carry it to their nest, eat the starch and leave the seed to germinate. It's only found at one location in the forest, and RBGE wanted to grow more. 'We tied a mesh like a little teabag over the flowers to catch the seeds when they fell,' Liz says. The seeds will be germinated and transplanted to new locations in the forest to make the population more resilient.

Having the Woodland Trust as a partner has helped ACF to build relationships with their neighbouring landowners. 'Partnerships mean that extreme views are tempered and we all have to find a way to collaborate,' says Henry. 'There is inevitably extra work in genuine engagement with the community, but this is definitely outweighed by the benefits.' And knowledge gained in this project can be shared. Achnacarry Estate and Forestry and Land Scotland are now joining in to form an ambitious landscape-scale collaboration. 'It felt a bit impertinent, trying to inspire more established neighbouring landowners to learn from us – the new kids in the Glen,' continues Henry. 'But I quickly realised that our neighbours took their role as custodians seriously. To be honest I think these ancient trees speak for themselves in inspiring landowners to restore these forests to their former glory.'

KNAPDALE

CHAPTER SIX

WETLAND

It's 8 o' clock on a May evening. I'm walking quietly around a wooded freshwater loch. Bluebells glow in the dappled shade and the wooden notes of a cuckoo echo from the hillside. I reach a hide – just a roof and wall to provide shelter from the Scottish weather, but on an evening like this a bit of weather is useful, to keep the midges at bay. Two people are here already, sitting by the shore in deckchairs. We greet each other in a whisper, and I also settle down to wait. Normally in Argyll you'd strike up a conversation, ask where they're from, but it's weird whispering in the ear of someone you've never met before, so we don't. A light breeze from the south ripples the water and blows away any perfume or rustling we might be producing, as well as the midges.

I've come here hoping to see the beavers. This loch is only five miles from my house, but in the 15 years since they were released here, I've only seen them once. It's easy to spot their presence – there are gnawed tree stumps all along the path – but to see these shy animals you have to make a special effort to come out at dusk on a summer evening.

Nothing happens for the first hour, nothing except a dabchick fishing between the waterlilies, the water rippling green with reflections from the oak forest. A buzzard soars above the treetops. Marsh marigold flowers shine brightly in the shallows and a sedge warbler sings its scratchy song from the reeds. It's lovely to have a reason to just sit and absorb it all. A huge pile of logs on the far bank looks to be where the beavers have built their lodge, so I keep checking it with my binoculars. I notice a floating log just offshore and check that too. It's a beaver! It must have swum there under water, and is lying flat on the surface, looking and listening for danger. Reassured, it swims back towards the lodge like a paddling terrier, and then curves underwater like a whale diving, its hips appearing above the surface but not the tail. The lodge entrance is underwater. Another animal appears, this one more ginger in colour. It swims up a channel and into the reed bed, off to look for some leaves or tree bark for its breakfast.

Tawny owls are starting to hoot from the shadows as we creep away, delighted with this glimpse of one of Scotland's rarest animals. But it wasn't always that way. Before the 1600s, Scotland was home to many beavers, which were valued by humans for their thick fur and for 'castoreum' (from the beaver's Latin name *Castor*). This 'exudate' is produced from beneath the tail of both sexes, and mixed with their urine to scent-mark their territory. Castoreum is used by perfumiers to provide the 'leathery' notes in a scent, and is still used today. The beavers were hunted to extinction, and the Scottish landscape had to manage without them for 400 years.

It has taken that long for us to realise that beavers are much more valuable alive than dead. As I was about to discover, their abilities as landscape engineers far outweigh their value as a perfume-production workforce. Although this book is about landscape restoration by communities of people, in this chapter it is the community of beavers who are doing the spade-work. But to start with, that was a problem. I remember when it was first proposed to reintroduce beavers to Argyll, there was uproar in the local papers. Since their extinction, humans had taken on many impressive projects of their own. In Argyll the Crinan Canal was excavated (by shovel). Wetlands were drained for farming and rivers were straightened to remove water as quickly as possible. Having gained control of the landscape, humans were reluctant to let go. Landowners were worried that their farmland would be flooded. The canal board was worried about springing a leak. Walkers were worried about footpaths being inundated. Anglers were worried that fish would be prevented from reaching spawning-grounds by beaver dams. The idea of letting an animal change our carefully curated landscape was frightening.

However, we've done such a great job of land management that wetlands are now a scarce resource. They're indispensable to absorb heavy rainfall, preventing flooding downstream. They also slow water down, which prevents erosion, and they filter it to clean out sediment. These are free ecosystem services, and it is the beavers who keep these services functioning. At the beginning of this century a trial was proposed to see if beavers and people could live side-by-side in a modern age where nature is supposed to confine itself to nature reserves. Knapdale in Argyll is surrounded by hills and sea, and as beavers can't live in salt water, it was chosen as the perfect location to constrain them naturally during the project.

[opposite] *Beaver and flowering bog bean*

In 2009 beavers were reintroduced to Knapdale by a partnership of the Royal Zoological Society of Scotland, the Scottish Wildlife Trust, and Forests and Land Scotland. Four families were brought from Norway, which is similar in climate and terrain to Knapdale. The beavers were also a fairly close genetic match to the former Scottish population. After six months of quarantine, 16 animals were released in three different family groups on three different lochs.

Despite living in Knapdale myself, I didn't pay much attention to the reintroduction, as the beavers didn't seem properly wild. Although there were no fences around them, I thought of them as zoo animals. But this all changed when I started researching this book. I met Pete Creech from the Argyll Beaver Centre, and was converted by his infectious enthusiasm and knowledge of the subject. Pete invited me on a walk around the lochs to show me how the beavers had settled back into their former haunts. As we walked down the track, we had to watch where we put our feet. The ground was covered in a moving carpet of thousands of tiny baby frogs, all hopping in the same direction. 'This lot have been going for five days,' said Pete, 'and it's all because of this wetland created by the beavers.'

All around the loch we can see trees felled with that classic 'chewed in the middle' shape. I ask Pete why beavers gnaw at trees. Are they eating the wood? He explains that they're not interested in eating the trunk. By felling the tree they can reach the fresh new twigs and leaves at the top. They then use the cut material to dam streams and expand the wetland, so they can swim into the flooded woods to reach new foraging grounds. They float foliage back to their lodge to feed their kits, or store the branches under water as a winter food supply. They don't hibernate, and in winter will even gather bare branches and chew off the bark, like a child nibbling chocolate from a Kit-Kat.

Pete has learned how to retain a little control. 'There's no point in ripping out a dam,' he says. 'The beavers will fight you all the way.' To protect forestry roads Pete has installed 'beaver deceivers'. These are pipes set at the required water-height that drain water past the dam. He has to keep an eye on them to make sure the beavers don't block them.

[opposite] *Beaver*

Pete knows many of the 30 animals by name. Bjornar and Millie are the most visible pair, and have held a territory for 13 years so far, which makes them long-lived for beavers in the wild. They have recently arrived from a neighbouring loch, but Bjornar had to construct the new lodge before the family could move. I'm amazed at the amount of pre-planning, as this new home is a kilometre away from their last residence. With their large round body, tiny eyes and expressionless faces, beavers don't look super-intelligent, but they obviously have more going on than I realised. Instinct is involved too – beavers kept as pets will gather cushions and pile them up around the house, even though there's no water around.

Pete talks me through the construction of a lodge. Bjornar will start by burrowing a hole underwater into the bank. He tunnels upwards until he is above water-level and digs out a chamber. He gathers branches from the forest, gnaws them into stakes and pushes them in around the entrance. Using his front paws more like hands than feet, he carries in armfuls of branches and interweaves them, plastering them with mud. More branches are piled on top, making the lodge safe from nearly all predators. Once he's dug more chambers for sleeping, the first space becomes a kind of utility room where the family can wash off mud and groom.

Only Millie, as the dominant female, will breed, although younger relatives stay in the family home and help out. Beavers mate in December and the kits are born in April. They stay protected in the lodge for two months until they are weaned, and stay with their family for two and a half years, learning how to refine their instincts for building and water engineering. As part of monitoring the reintroduction, Pete and his co-worker Oly Hemmings have set cameras all over the area to check that the animals remain healthy. It also allows them to witness family life. Pete told me about watching the babies, called kits, try to dive. They have too much air in their fur compared to their body mass, and tip upside down with their bottoms in the air when they try. One of their favourite foods is rowan leaves. The adults bring back rowan branches and the kits roll up the leaves like cigars and stuff them into their mouths.

[opposite] *Frog and frogspawn*

Beavers are great landscape engineers. 'Owen is a construction-orientated beaver,' says Pete. 'He builds dams and sub-dams.' Owen monitors the water levels, raising or lowering them as necessary. Pete shows me a new dam 5 feet high, made with branches and rocks, and forming a new pool behind it where whirligig beetles are already spinning. These pools, meres and rivulets create homes for frogs, newts and dragonflies. The coppiced tree stumps produce new fresh growth, and the dappled shade is perfect for salmon and trout fry. They can warm in the sun or move to the shade when it's too hot.

Every two to four years each beaver family moves to a different loch. When the dams are no longer maintained, water levels fall and silt is deposited to fertilise the ground, creating fresh new growth known as a 'beaver meadow'. Marsh marigolds flourish. Vegetation can recover and tree stumps regenerate, as long as deer are not too numerous. They love the fresh leaves and grass. The cyclical land-use creates variety, which is always good for biodiversity.

The lochs here are nutrient-poor. The woodchips that fall into the water grow algae, providing food for tadpoles. One of the trail-cams caught footage of a mallard teaching her ducklings to catch them. Other waterbirds like mute swans benefit from the higher water levels, as their nests remain safe from predators.

Eels also thrive. They provide food for otters and herons, and Pete watched a heron catching them on the remote camera. The writhing eel wrapped itself around the bird's beak, and once swallowed, continued wriggling in its throat. Eels breed in the Sargasso Sea off South America. They start as a leaf-shaped animal that can drift on the current, then metamorphose into silver elvers and make their way up all the rivers of Europe. Beaver dams are porous, so they can wriggle through to live in the flooded areas behind. They feed and grow, eating dragonfly larvae and small fish. After maybe 15 years they make their way back across the ocean to breed. They are one of our most threatened species. 'When I was a kid, eels were so common that the pubs on the River Severn held eel-drinking competitions – how quickly someone can drink a pint of live elvers,' says Pete. 'Now, kilo for kilo, elvers are more valuable than cocaine.'

[opposite] *Marsh marigolds and roe deer*

I want to find out about other wildlife that benefits from the wetlands, and Pete puts me in touch with Pat Batty. She did a lot of the official dragonfly monitoring as part of the reintroduction, and is the Scottish recorder for the British Dragonfly Society. I invite her and her husband Dave to my house for a coffee. She's now a retired teacher, but started getting interested in dragonflies when she was a new parent. 'It was easy to do with wee kids in tow,' she says. When she went back to work, she encouraged lots of Argyll schools to create ponds in their grounds as a way of engaging the children with wildlife.

Pat offers to survey my garden pond. It's an overcast day and breezy, but she explains that we don't need to see the adults. They are only the final egg-laying phase of a dragonfly's life. The larvae live underwater for several years, but only fly as adults for a few weeks. As she goes to fetch her equipment from the car, Dave tells me, 'She's very modest, but actually I think she knows more about Scottish dragonflies than anyone.' Pat returns with her high-tech equipment, a plastic colander and a white ice-cream tub. 'Let's go for a guddle,' she says. She scoops up mud and water, and soon she is grinning. 'How long ago did you make this pond? We've got four species already, as well as newts and tadpoles.' Looking in the white tub, I can see two basic body-types. The smaller damselfly larvae wriggle their long tails like a fish to swim through the water. The rounded dragonfly larvae scuttle across the bottom. Pat shows me how to identify them using a 10x hand-lens. We find a common darter (with lateral spines), a blue-tailed damselfly (that breathes through three spikes, or lamellae, on its tail), a four-spotted chaser (with pointed abdomen and yellow face-stripes) and an azure damselfly (with spots on the head). 'When I'm doing this with kids I have to watch that they don't put the larvae in with tadpoles, as they eat everything,' says Pat. Both the larvae and adults are predators, with big hinged jaws that can shoot out to grab prey. The adults have the added advantage of speed, and their wings work independently, which makes them very manoeuvrable. 'They're like a combination of an attack helicopter and a fighter jet.'

Surveying dragonflies is a great way of monitoring the health of a wetland community. 'Dragonflies are easy to study,' Pat tells me, 'because there are only 25 species in Scotland.' Four new species have arrived this century as species move northwards with global warming. In Argyll we have 19 species, as there is such a varied landscape of mountains, bogs and islands. There is a dragonfly for every habitat-type in Scotland, even woodland, as long as there is some sort of water. Some species are very particular. Beautiful demoiselles like fast flowing water with a few trees to create dappled sunlight.

We put on our wellies and go to a boggy area at the edge of our village. I'm glad I'm with an expert, as I struggle to identify dragonflies, especially when they whizz past at top speed. Pat explains that, as with birds, behaviour is also important. 'Northern damselfly will follow the vegetation around a pond, while common blue damselfly will be out over the open water.' She shows me where to look for different larvae. We find keeled skimmers in a flowing burn, four-spotted chasers in a mossy puddle, and the monster larva of a golden ringed dragonfly which takes five years to develop.

When Pat started 40 years ago, not much was known about Scottish dragonflies. Learning about the larvae was important for survey work, as some adults have very short flight times and could be missed. Also, seeing an adult doesn't prove breeding, as it could have flown in. Scottish records go back to Victorian times, often centring on railway stations, from where the entomologists could access more remote locations. As knowledge of dragonflies increases, it's easier to protect them. For some species it's enough to dig new ponds, which can act as stepping stones to connect populations. Pat encourages everyone to submit photos online to the British Dragonfly Society, who will help with identification.

At first, Pat was worried about the beaver reintroduction. Dragonflies lay their eggs on waterside vegetation or underneath floating water plants. The Knapdale location was chosen because the beavers were contained, but if the population grew too much, they might eat all the aquatic vegetation. Fifteen years on, Pat believes that in Scotland as a whole the benefits of these grazers balances any negative effects. Their grazing stops wetlands filling in, and their habit of moving location every few years allows areas to recover.

Anglers were also concerned about the return of the beavers, worrying that they might block rivers for migrating fish. However, as Pete points out, there are 70,000 beavers in Norway, on some of the best salmon rivers in the world. Fifteen years on, the fishermen have been won over. In times of flood and drought, river flow

has been evened out, the water is cleaner, there are more insects for food and the size of fish has increased. There's been a lot of work recently to make rivers into better habitats; to restore meandering curves (sinuation) and add dead wood to prevent erosion, but beavers do all this river restoration for free. In this chapter it is the beavers who are restoring the habitat for the benefit of the human community. Opponents of the beavers sometimes point to the trouble caused by beavers in Patagonia who've escaped from fur farms, but trees in South America haven't evolved with beavers. European trees have learned to regrow when nibbled, in a coppicing reaction.

In 2024 it's 15 years since the beavers' return, and Pete and Oly have engaged with 30,000 people in that time. Tourists stay in local hotels and build their holiday around a guided walk, so beavers have brought economic benefits too. Under a community asset transfer scheme, Pete and Oly have taken on former forestry buildings to run as a visitor centre. I ask Pete about the most common reactions to the beavers. He says firstly people are surprised by how big they are. They also assume that beavers eat fish, though in fact they are completely vegetarian. He explains to visitors how adapted beavers are to their watery world. They have a membrane that can close across their eyes 'which acts like swimming goggles'. They have an incredibly wide gape, and front teeth that continue to grow. These teeth look bright orange, because they are strengthened with iron to make them strong enough to chew through a tree trunk. They can close their mouth behind these teeth so they can chew under water. And of course there's the beaver's most characteristic feature, its broad paddle of a tail with its strange leathery, scaly appearance.

In 2016 the Scottish Government decided the beavers were an asset to the landscape and could stay. They were declared a native species, and new individuals were released to prevent inbreeding. As I've discovered, they are animals right at the heart of their community. The landscape hadn't made sense without them, and now I was seeing it as it was meant to be.

[opposite] *Demoiselle damselflies*

DUMFRIES

CHAPTER SEVEN

RIVER

It's September, and a female salmon swims through the wide estuary of the Solway Firth, hugging the coast. Since she was last here four years ago, she's travelled 3,000 kilometres to the Norwegian Sea and back. She was feeding north of the Arctic Circle on oil-rich sand eels and other small fish, and she now weighs 15 pounds. She's used the magnetic field of the earth and her memory of currents and tides to migrate back to the place of her birth in the south of Scotland. Her silvery body is sleek and designed for long-distance travel. Her white belly has hidden her against the light of the sky, to avoid marine predators such as dolphins and seals. Her siblings may have been caught by fishing trawlers or died for lack of food, but she is lucky enough to be returning home.

She is following the faint but familiar taste of her birthplace, the River Nith: a particular combination of minerals and acidity, of autumn leaves, grass from river meadows and the tang of peat from mountain streams. She passes wooden stakes in the estuarine mud where the nets used to catch thousands of fish every year. There are so few salmon now that this fishery no longer exists. Haaf-netting, a traditional hand-netting fishery started here a thousand years ago by the Vikings, has also declined for lack of salmon.

As she enters the river with its wide mudbanks, she ignores any food carried by the current. Her body is changing and she's no longer interested in feeding. She needs to reach the head of the river where she can lay her eggs in the relative safety of shallow water. Twelve kilometres upstream is the town of Dumfries. She tastes rain-washed tyre-rubber from the roads and plastic crisp packets. This is where the sea loses its influence and the river turns from brine to fresh water. Heavy showers mean the river is in spate, so it's easy for her to leap over the historic weir that spans the river. A century ago, council employees would net salmon here to feed the town. Now she slips unmolested beneath the ancient Devorgilla Bridge.

The lowlands of Dumfries and Galloway are farming country. Swimming upstream she tastes cow-dung and artificial fertiliser. Her body changes from silver to brown, blending with the river. Her belly becomes bloated with developing eggs. There are anglers on the banks, fishing with brightly-coloured feather flies.

She moves swiftly onwards, ignoring the temptation. Despite not wanting to feed, other fish fail to resist the lures, in the way that a cat can't resist jumping on a toy mouse. Any fish caught are returned alive to the river now, as they are too precious to kill.

Leaving the main river, she navigates into her home tributary. The water is shallow now, but she can hide in deep pools, waiting for a downpour that will make the last few miles of river passable. In early December her moment comes and she dashes upstream with a male salmon who has been following her scent. She chooses a bed of gravel where the water flows fast enough to carry away stones that she dislodges with her tail. This shallow depression, called a 'redd', is where she lays her eggs. The male, holding his place next to her, almost without effort in the fast current, releases a cloud of 'milt' to fertilise the eggs. She then moves upstream to dislodge more pebbles to bury them. She produces as many as 12,000 eggs. Many will be lost. They will feed eels, trout, and birds like dippers.

The scales of a salmon have growth rings like a tree. Narrow rings record her hungry river days, whilst wider bands show months of good feeding in the ocean. Our female is weak from lack of food, but if she can make it back to the sea, there's a chance that she might make this journey again. Some fish, exhausted from their efforts, will certainly die here, releasing the nutrients that their bodies have carried from the sea to the mountains. This enriches the river, so helping the next generation of salmon.

In the twenty-first century, numbers of salmon have plummeted in all the rivers on the west coast. In 2008 the declared rod-catch on the River Nith was 4,500 salmon, but in 2023, only 400 adult fish were caught. How can it be that such an emblematic Scottish animal is on the brink of extinction? Surely the causes of such catastrophic decline should be obvious? The Nith District Salmon Fishery Board is funded by the local fishing community to maintain the health of the river. The current director of the Board is Jim Henderson, and he needs to find out why salmon numbers are plummeting. 'The Nith is a 1,500 square mile salmon-producing factory,' he tells me.

He has been putting out fish traps to compare the numbers of young fish, or smolt, in different tributaries, and invites me along. 'I want to know why one tributary rears 5,000 smolt and another only 53.' En route, Jim drives me via

Wanlockhead, the highest village in Scotland. For centuries this was an important lead-mining area. It also produced some of the world's purest gold. For such a tiny place, it has a surprisingly well-populated graveyard. There are mining spoil heaps scattered across the hillside, and gravel from them has been washed into the river by the rain. This makes it a perfect place for salmon to lay their eggs. Jim shows me where he has seen a 24-pound salmon, its back rising out of the water of a stream that's only an arm's width across. It had raced upstream to breed, but was caught out by a cold night when the water froze, cutting it off from retreat.

Egg development is closely linked to the temperature of the surrounding water. The eggs are laid around December but hatching won't occur until spring when the water temperatures increase. From fertilisation to hatching takes 450 degree-days. This means that in a constant temperature of 10°C, it would take 45 days. The young fish live as parr for two or three years, depending on food availability, then one year in early May their bodies change. They lose the stripes which camouflage them against the river bed, and become silvery smolt. Instead of swimming against the current, waiting for food to be brought down river, their instincts tell them to turn and swim downstream towards the sea. And this is how we are hoping to catch them.

Jim has set netting across the river to guide the smolts via a funnel into a metal tank. We lift the lid, but it's not easy to spot them in the swirling water. Scooping them into a bucket, Jim tells me they are trout and salmon, but they are all red-and-black-spotted and look the same to me. He points out the subtle differences, revealing how salmon are better designed for long-distance travel. They are sleeker, with a narrower 'wrist' before the tail, which is more deeply forked. Larger pectoral fins drive them forward. Identification is confirmed by the single black spot on the gill-cover of the salmon, and the red adipose fin on the trout. He measures and weighs the six trout and 12 salmon and releases them.

As well as knowing how many smolts are produced, Jim wants to know what happens to them as they travel downstream. They face threats from predators, from water pollution and starvation. In 2021 his team caught 150 smolts, and these were fitted with tiny electronic tracking devices. They placed eight acoustic receivers along the length of the river, especially where they thought the fish might encounter problems. They discovered that the smolts almost always travelled at night to avoid predators. Almost half of the tagged fish made it from the headwaters to the sea, a distance of 56 kilometres, taking them on average 18 days.

But the project didn't end there. It fed into an ambitious three-year study organised by the Atlantic Salmon Trust. The West Coast Salmon Smolt Tracking Project aims to find out why Atlantic salmon have declined by 70 per cent in the first quarter of the twenty-first century. This collaboration with government agencies and the University of Glasgow has tagged more than a 1,000 smolts from ten rivers on the west coast of Scotland. Over 200 acoustic receivers were positioned between the peninsulas and islands of the west coast to ascertain the exact migration corridors used by the fish.

The smolts all headed west and then north to feed on krill in Arctic waters. 'I loved seeing a smolt, that I'd caught in the Nith, ping the receiver off the west coast of Scotland,' says Jim. Data from the project showed that there was not one migration corridor that was used by all salmon. This matches with their other behaviour; salmon have survived by having lots of variety in their life cycle. Different individuals lay eggs in early autumn or deepest winter. The young salmon grow in the river for one, two or three years, transitioning from fry to parr. At any one time, the river's community isn't just within the river, so one pollution event won't kill the whole population.

So could it be conditions at sea that are decimating the salmon population? It seems that populations of krill and sand eels are moving north with global warming, and fish may have further to swim to find food. They are also affected by high infestations of sea lice from the many fish farms that have sprung up in our sea lochs.

When Jim started in fisheries management 40 years ago, the qualifications for the job were very different. 'In those days you had to be over six feet tall and "capable",' he tells me. When he started as a bailiff, aged 19, the Nith was one of the most heavily poached rivers in Scotland. 'The level of violence then – you've no idea,' he

[opposite] *Grey wagtail*

laughs. Poaching was big business, with refrigerated lorries being used to take away fish by the tonne. Jim threw himself into protecting the salmon. I suspect that as a young man he enjoyed the adrenaline rush when leaping into a river at night to arrest poachers. His theory was that if he always worked harder than the poachers, then word would get out that it was too much trouble to poach the Nith, and they would go elsewhere. He got to know the river intimately. Lying under a bush in the dark he could tell if an oystercatcher alarm call signalled a hunting otter or a group of men. In his worst year he took 103 people to court. Jim had death threats and police protection, and I ask if he still feels threatened. 'If I walked into a pub now, some of those men would buy me a drink. Nowadays there are other ways to make quick money. £10,000 of cocaine is a lot easier to carry than £10,000 of salmon. And there aren't enough salmon left to make poaching worthwhile.'

Legislation requiring restaurants to prove the provenance of the fish on their menu also put a stop to poaching. Farmed salmon, despite its environmental problems, has had the benefit of providing an alternative. 'Now salmon is cheaper than cheese,' says Jim.

He decided to learn more about the river he was looking after, and took an Open University degree. It was tough in more ways than one. 'Studying environmental science gave me the feeling that we were all doomed – that we might as well give up and go home.' Considering the scale of problems faced by salmon, it would be easy to shrug and give up, but that's not the sort of person Jim is. If he can't protect the salmon once they leave his river, he can make sure that when they do leave, they are in the best possible condition to withstand the threats they will face.

As Jim drives me around the Nith tributaries, we spot sand martins feeding on insects emerging from the river. They are nesting in holes where the river has eroded a steep bank. With heavier rainfall from global warming, the river has more energy, cutting out a wider, shallower bed. As summers become hotter, the shallow water could heat to more than 20°C – dangerous for developing fish. Jim would like to plant trees to shade the river, but it's not his land. The riverbank provides rare flat ground that's valuable for lambing. He's persuaded the farmer to lose part of his grazing land to trees, because the tree roots will reduce the erosion.

Jim shows me where he has already planted alder, silver birch, hawthorn and even Scots pine. Insects falling from the leaves will provide extra food for the fish. The leaves themselves will add nutrients to the river when they fall in autumn. But for the trees to grow, Jim needed to pay for fencing. Funding came from an XE racing legacy project. Jim can tell from the blank look on my face that I have no idea what that means. Apparently XE refers to extreme electric cars that race off-road. Legacy funding is a part of all their events, and so when an abandoned coal mine in the Nith catchment area hosted a race, money became available. He's happy to facilitate an environmental project which will benefit the salmon. 'I don't care who pays for it,' he laughs. 'Do you know how much all that fencing costs?' It's also good publicity, he says. 'When you've got a racing driver standing next to you with his arm around your shoulder, people pay you more attention.'

Jim has also worked with industry to preserve, or even improve the flow of a river. Mining operations or the installation of windfarm electricity cables sometimes require a waterway to be moved. He has learned how to partner with the river to create more variety in water flow. Adding curves or sinuosity gives variety – slow and fast water, riffles, runs and deeper pools where the fish can hide. Large boulders, in the right place, force the water to do the heavy lifting and sculpt the river bed. Tree roots in the bank stop the river going off piste. And other species benefit too. 'I get a kick out of seeing a bird nesting in a tree that I planted 30 years ago,' he says.

Trout live in the same rivers as salmon and face the same threats. They are generally smaller, and permits to fish for them are less expensive. They are 'partially anadromous', i.e. some adapt to live in salt water and become sea trout for part of their lives, while others stay in the river as brown trout. My husband, Mark, is obsessed with fly-fishing for trout, and I ask him to teach me, although I have to say I'm a bit conflicted. Catching fish that I'm going to eat seems to me a valid way of interacting with the natural world. But now that fish are so rare that we have to release them back into the river, is it possible to justify catching fish just for entertainment?

[following pages] *Atlantic salmon in the river.*

Mark ties his own flies with equipment inherited from his father and grandfather. Traditionally these are tied from natural materials, and are designed to mimic the insects that the fish are eating. Like any sport, there is always shiny new merchandise on offer. Glittering tinsel and fluorescent threads don't seem very river-friendly, and I don't want to use factory-farmed animals either. Luckily Mark is already thinking this way. When we're driving and we find road-kill squirrel or a dead bird, he'll take it home for its fur or feathers.

We make the lure on a barbless hook. This is more difficult to fish with, but is less damaging to the fish as it's easy to remove. I tie my first fly using a feather called CDC. This Cul de Canard feather is from the preen-gland on a duck's bottom, and is so fluffy that it traps air and floats, mimicking the wings of an 'emerger': an aquatic insect that is pushing out of its larval skin, ready to launch into the air. We make another fly with the twisted hackle-feather of a cockerel. The body is from rabbit fur and the legs from the dark hairs on a hare's ear. This one is designed to sit on top of the water like an egg-laying adult fly. Mark looks critically at my efforts. 'The best flies are insubstantial, like an insect,' he says. Mine is quite chunky, but it will have to do. When Mark is fly-tying I keep finding glasses full of water on the table. He drops the fly onto the surface and looks at it from below to check the silhouette from a trout's point of view.

Fly-tying requires an intimacy with nature that was more common when Mark's grandfather was alive. The fly called 'Tup's Indispensable' is made using the soft hair from a ram's testicles.

One evening Mark takes me to fish on his favourite trout river. Looking over the bridge, we can see their dark speckled silhouettes lazily holding position in the current. In the leaf-sprouting hawthorns, a blackcap is singing, its liquid song flowing alongside the river. Wood anemones are nodding their white flowers in the dappled shade. A dipper flies upstream with a beak full of food and disappears under the bridge. It will have a mossy nest, full of chicks, hidden there. It reappears, landing on a stone in the river – a bulky brown bird with a white bib. After bobbing a few times, it slides gently under the surface as if there was no divide between

[opposite] *Kingfisher*

the worlds of air and water. We watch it swimming about in the rushing stream hunting for insects, like an underwater blackbird.

Mark wades into the river and lifts out a stone covered in hundreds of tiny tubes – the homes of caddis-fly larvae, trout food. In their current form they would make a gritty mouthful, as each has protected itself with a house of tiny stones from the riverbed. But to complete their life cycle they must hatch from bottom-dwelling worm to flying insect, and then they are vulnerable. Their survival strategy is to hatch in large groups, following a cue of temperature or day-length, so that a few of the thousands will escape the predators.

There is a line of bubbles and detritus floating downstream which Mark calls (rather unappealingly) the scum line. The biggest fish situate themselves under this food conveyor belt but safely tucked beneath overhanging tree roots or branches. Smaller fish hide in the white water at the top of a pool. They must expend more energy to stay in the current but have first dibs on any food washed downstream. 'The days you live for are those when a big hatch is on,' says Mark. 'For half-an hour there will be clouds of flies coming up the river and even the big fish come out from under the bank to feed.' I can see that for him, the fieldcraft needed for fishing is very similar to that of wildlife-filmmaking: watching the animals and working out their behaviour.

Fishing requires a good understanding of entomology. You need to work out which insects will be hatching at what time of day or which month of the year. This can be a community effort. If another fisherman walks past, he'll ask, 'Any luck?' I've noticed the answer is never 'No.' Mark will say 'Only a couple,' or something incomprehensible (to me), like 'I've had no luck on the dry so I'm going to give the euro nymphing a go.' Sometimes the fishermen will get out their boxes of flies and compare which ones have been most successful today, maybe an APT or a DHE. (That's an All-Purpose Terrestrial or a Deer Hair Emerger.)

Mark shows me how to cast the line, flicking it across the river so the fly lands lightly on the water. I'm aiming for a spot just upstream from where a fish has been rising to take real flies. I have to let the lure drift with the current, not being

[opposite] *Dipper*

dragged by the line behind it. I feel a small pull as the fish tastes the fly, but it's obviously not convinced by my fly-tying abilities and spits it out. Mark has a go and brings in a beautiful little trout, dotted with red and black spots. He scoops it in his net, unhooks it and releases it back into the current.

The buzz of catching a big fish is a big part of why Mark goes fishing, but I'm not so fussed about that adrenaline rush. I realise that I'm just as happy to sit on the bank sketching amongst the smell of water mint and the burbling of the river as it runs over stones. (Interestingly, in all my years of hanging around on river banks, I've never encountered a fisherwoman.) As well as the thrill of the chase, another big part of the fishing experience is having a reason to be outside in a beautiful place. It's similar to sketching, in that the wildlife forgets that you're there. Mark tells me about some of the extraordinary experiences he's had. Kingfishers dive for fish right next to him. One evening at dusk an otter hunted just feet away between him and the bank. 'I could look down on it through the water, hunting among tree roots,' he told me. He saw a red squirrel too. 'I thought it was coming down to drink, but it swam across the river to a branch hanging in the water and climbed up into the tree. I didn't know they could swim.'

On the River Nith, it's the salmon that brings the community together. Every spring Jim Henderson organises a ceremony for the opening of the fishing season. There are speeches, toasts with local whisky, and a bagpiper. Jim has been head-hunted by some very wealthy east coast rivers, but he's committed to the Nith, and is doing all he can to maintain salmon numbers there. The steep decline has been levelled out by the fact that the fish are no longer taken for eating. Stake-net fishing out in the estuary, which dates from 1868, has had to stop, with the loss of all the associated culture. Fishermen must return their catches. But these measures are now used up, and so the fishing community must keep identifying problems and finding solutions.

Jim's team regularly sample the numbers of aquatic insects in the river to make sure there is enough food for the fish. A recent, frightening threat to river health is the flea and tick collars worn by many dogs, which contain powerful insecticides. When dogs swim in the river in hot weather, these chemicals wash into the water and can drastically reduce numbers of invertebrates.

'If salmon had legs and fur, my job would be a lot easier,' Jim tells me. He is encouraging a new generation of fishing enthusiasts by running free fishing days for school children. If they can feel that same passion that Jim felt when his uncle first took him fishing, then the river may have a future. I feel that the reason we treat the natural world with so little respect, is that we no longer really know it. Whatever you might think of catching fish for sport rather than the pot, it is the community of fishermen who understand the river. When the river is used for sewage disposal, or when water is siphoned off for irrigation, it is the anglers who notice. They bring money into the area via hotels and hospitality, and pay for river management via the fishing permit fees. Without fishing, money for managing the river, and keeping it healthy, would drain away.

ARGYLL COAST & ISLANDS HOPE SPOT

CHAPTER EIGHT

COAST

At university I did a zoology degree, and on one field course we studied the seashore. We learned to survey wildlife using quadrats and transects, but it was a very underwhelming experience. The seaweed was dark and shrivelled, mussels were clamped shut and anemones were dark red blobs, waiting for the tide to return. We never got into the water, for obvious reasons: it's cold, wet and potentially dangerous. I've always found the sea a little scary. Growing up on the south coast of England with the big waves of the English Channel crashing onto steep pebble beaches, the water was intimidating, but in Scotland the ocean swell is blocked by offshore islands. The water here is cold enough to justify a wetsuit, which somehow feels more protective. And then I met Lottie, whose passion for cold-water swimming, knowledge of local tides and currents, and enthusiasm for underwater wildlife, converted me. When I finally put on a mask and stuck my head under the surface, I couldn't believe that I'd been living right next to this amazing world for so long, completely unaware.

I'll try and describe a swim we had in one of the many sea lochs on the Sound of Jura, but it's hard to do it justice. Lottie swims every day of the year, but I prefer a sunny day when the underwater colours glow and the shallows are almost warm. Pulling on all the neoprene is hot work; the wetsuit is tight, the hood makes me deaf, the gloves fumble the straps of the mask which steams up as I overheat. It's a relief to get in the water, floating in the shallows, putting my head under and trying to slow my nervous breathing through the snorkel. As soon as I start looking around, I relax. A tiny pipefish, like seaweed with an eye, hangs quizzically in front of me. Sunlight dapples the sand where intriguing tentacles flicker. I waft away the sand grains and reveal a dahlia anemone, like a candy-striped flower, buried there.

We push off and let the tide take us. The current is strong but completely predictable, so we know where to catch a ride and where to jump off into a back eddy. As we fly across the landscape, crabs scuttle for cover below. We're accompanied by our own squadron of fish, darting through the current beside us – corkwing wrasse. The large males are striped blue and red, and defend a nest they've tucked between the rocks.

Starfish, sea urchin and shore crab

We glide over a forest of sea oak which billows in the current. Lottie points out sugar kelp, fringed with shirt-ruffles. She's a seaweed expert, harvesting it for food (this kelp is an ingredient in miso soup) and making beautiful artwork by drying and pressing it. She's the perfect companion. As the seaweed is pushed and pulled by the tide, we catch tantalising glimpses of a hidden world below. I part the strands to reveal mesmerising combinations of colour and texture. A tiny blue starfish rests on a cushion of orange sponge. Translucent seasquirts containing bright yellow coils shine like miniature light bulbs. Crusty pink maerl coral glows pale against the turquoise depths. Sgraffito layers of bryozoans encrust the rocks, animated by the rippling sunlight. We arrive at an open glade in the sea oak and several large mullet dash for cover, making us both jump. Tucked under boulders we spot tall apricot plumose anemones with feather-boa frills draped around their shoulders. We hold on to the rock as if in a strong headwind, then let go to soar and tumble in an exhilarating ride as the ground drops away below.

Having (mostly) conquered my fear of the unknown, I have one remaining worry, which is how cold I can let myself become. I'm shivering, but it's hard to tell if it's from cold or excitement. It's addictive, wanting to know what new amazing experience is waiting around each corner, but eventually I head for shore. I float in as far as I possibly can, as even in a foot of water there are brittlestars and I don't want to crush them.

Most people have never taken a look under the surface of the sea, for the same reasons as I didn't for so long. This 'out of sight out of mind' situation has meant that traditionally our coastal waters have been treated as a free waste-disposal system. Five hundred years ago this wasn't a problem, but since then, Scotland's population has increased tenfold. This means more human sewage, more intensive agriculture and more factory-farming. There's a bigger profit to be made if waste can be dumped where no-one notices it. It's only when surfers become sick, when sanitary products wash up on beaches, and when wild salmon become covered in sea lice from fish farms, that we start to realise what has been happening.

The seabed is owned by Crown Estate Scotland for 12 nautical miles off the west coast. The reigning monarch can't sell it or benefit from any revenue; all profit goes to the Scottish Government for public spending. Scotland's coastal waters are managed by the Government's Marine Directorate. Seafood is one of our largest exports, and is worth billions of pounds. An independent Scotland would need to be financially self-sufficient, and so for the SNP Government there is an incentive to encourage fishing and fish-farming industries to make the country financially secure.

Creel fisherman catch lobsters, crabs and langoustines, which are mostly driven in refrigerated lorries to European markets. Scallops can either be hand-dived, a sustainable practice, or they can be dredged. Dredging involves raking up all life on the seabed and discarding everything except the scallops. Most people, including the fishermen themselves, never see the effects of this process, and that is probably why it still continues. Until the 1980s this damaging practice was only allowed three miles off-shore, but when the Thatcher government changed this, coastal ecosystems were destroyed.

This is all depressing stuff. In the last few years many communities on the west coast have become so fed-up with misuse of their waters that local organisations have sprung up to take action. Volunteers have taken on causes that they feel passionate about or to which they can contribute expertise. Some want to clean up plastic pollution from their beaches. Some lobby government on the effect of fish-farm parasites on local wild salmon and sea trout. Some have campaigned against deafening 'acoustic deterrents' that keep seals away from fish farms, but also affect dolphins and porpoises. Others campaign to reinstate the three-mile limit. There are now over 20 of these groups, and a wonderful umbrella organisation, Coastal Communities Network Scotland, has started up to connect and support them; a community of communities!

I belong to one of these groups, called Friends of the Sound of Jura, led by film-maker John Aitchison. It was formed to campaign against a proposed fish farm near the mouth of the River Add. Sea trout and salmon numbers have plummeted here for many of the reasons discussed in the River chapter, and we worried that this poorly-sited farm would be the final straw. The campaign was successful, but it's hard to continue battling against such massive vested interests, especially when you're doing it in your spare time.

The legendary American marine biologist Sylvia Earle chose to work for positive outcomes for marine environments and had the idea of creating 'Hope Spots'. Her organisation, Mission Blue, inspires public awareness through a network of the most important marine areas on the planet. Four Argyll groups came together and successfully applied for Hope Spot status to be awarded to our local coastline, the first in mainland UK. The Argyll Coasts and Islands Hope Spot was accredited for its great variety of habitats, from the shallow lagoons of Loch Sween to the deep canyon of the Sound of Jura and the Corryvrekan whirlpool. It is home to the 2-metre wide, endangered flapper skate. But there's no point having a Hope Spot if no-one knows about it. And how do you engage the public with wildlife that they can never experience?

Marine images of mine that sell are of animals that people recognise – like lobsters, mussels or mackerel. Eating seafood is an important way of connecting with and valuing the sea, but what about all the other amazing creatures? When you walk through a mature woodland with trees that have lived there for centuries, with lichen and mosses and ferns that grow alongside them, and with insects and bird life that depend on them, it is obvious that you are in a special place. But what about the underwater equivalent? If you haven't experienced it, why would you be motivated to protect it?

I'm a member of the Society of Wildlife Artists (SWLA), some of whose members had received dive-training, under a bursary from the Wildlife Trusts, to solve this very problem. In 2021 I invited a group of these artists to visit the Hope Spot for a week, to snorkel and draw underwater and share their experience. I had no budget to make this happen, but everyone signed up for the craziness of the idea. Lottie helped as a safety swimmer, Mark agreed to cook for everyone and my daughter made high-energy snacks for when the famished swimmers needed refuelling. My neighbour offered extra beds and everyone paid for their own travel.

We had a ball, despite the many challenges. All the normal rules of artwork are turned upside down underwater. There was no horizon, as we were looking down on the landscape. There was so much to see, most of which we couldn't distinguish as animal or plant, let alone identify.

The subjects were moving, we were also being pushed by the current, and anything loose floated away. We experimented with materials, tying our drawing boards around our waists so as to have both hands free for swimming, and knotting crayons and pencils onto elastic strings. We found that shiny paper or gesso-coated hardboard didn't disintegrate underwater. The drawings we made forced us to look closely and provided an aid to memory. Once ashore, dry and refuelled with chocolate brownies, we got out the paints and worked up ideas.

At the annual SWLA exhibition at the Mall Galleries in London we exhibited our field sketches. The energy and excitement of the work impressed marine biologist Miranda Krestovnikoff. She thought that drawing underwater was a mad enough idea to catch media attention, so she pitched the idea to the BBC's One Show. This gave us another reason to repeat it the following year. By this time, the Argyll Hope Spot had a project coordinator, Keira Anderson, who had the great idea that we should select local artists with access to their own local audiences. Over 30 people applied, and as well as painters we selected a musician, a jeweller, a podcaster, a printmaker, a photographer, a writer and a tattoo artist. These people were less experienced swimmers, and so Dan the Merman came onboard.

Dan is an open-water swim coach. His mum had been terrified of swimming, and teaching her had inspired him to give others the gift of confidence in the sea. His approach was holistic, and he taught us to be aware of our surroundings, of the weather and sea-state, as well as our breathing.

The final member of our team was Louise Scammell, an artist from Devon who was on the first year's residency. I had been worried that our wildlife wouldn't be as exciting as that on her home shores, but Louise was blown away by what she discovered, and was happy to come back as a tutor. She had a good camera set-up, and understood what she was looking at. Each evening she would show us photos of what she'd seen, so we knew what to search for. My instinct was always to swim too fast because of the cold water and nervousness, but she taught me to slow down and observe fish behaviour in the same way as I would watch birds.

[opposite] *Mussels and brittle stars*

Louise taught us about tiny, colourful sea-slugs, and which jellyfish to watch out for. The huge barrel jellyfish are gentle giants, and the shoals of pink moon jellies can be swum through, a mind-blowing 3D experience. The compass jellies are beautifully patterned, but the only one to avoid is the lion's mane jellyfish with its painful sting. (It used to be said that urine would neutralise a sting, but it's much better to rinse it with seawater, as fresh water or pee can make the pain worse.) Louise also inspired us with stories of her marine experiences, like the time she made a puffin-model hat to be able to approach the birds in the sea. She was entranced by seeing them 'fly' underwater, and by the silver rain of their fish-scale poo.

The day of filming for the One Show was wet and windy, but as we were all getting wet anyway it didn't matter. In the afternoon we sheltered in the village hall and made a collaborative artwork, a long banner where everyone shared their favourite experiences of the week. We used the banner at an open day for politicians and the public, to share what we'd found in the Hope Spot. All the great publicity meant we were getting requests for another residency.

Almost 60 people applied for our third underwater drawing week in 2023. Many of them were much more experienced marine biologists than me, but they wanted to learn about how we were engaging the public with marine conservation. We were invited to base ourselves for the week at the Kilchoan Estate on Loch Melfort. This estate is working towards ecological regeneration, this time privately funded by the owners. They are seeking to restore both land and sea together, and employ a marine rewilding officer, Marnik van Cauter. He arranged accommodation for our snorkellers, and allowed us to use the jetty and boathouse. He also provided my highlight of the week when he came back from checking his lobster pots with an octopus! We had salt-water tanks set up on the shore, and it was amazing to watch the animal climb around the aquarium with its suckered arms, changing colour and shape according to its mood. Octopuses are well-known for their intelligence. They pilfer shellfish from creels, and have learned to follow the ropes from one pot to the next, so are disliked by fishermen. Once we'd made drawings we returned the animal to the sea.

[opposite] *Curled octopus*

Outside Loch Melfort, in the Sound of Jura, there is a Marine Protected Area (MPA) designated to protect the flapper skate. These huge triangular fish were once called common skate, but now have been fished to very low numbers. Until recently it was unknown where they laid their eggs. The egg-cases, bigger than my hand and textured like golden tree-bark, occasionally wash ashore. We called them mermaid's purses when I was a kid. Marnik found a record from 1996 of a cluster of eggs found by divers in Loch Melfort. He surveyed the area in 2021 with divers from Open Seas and Shark and Skate Scotland, and was delighted to find an egg-laying site amongst boulders. The team were able to count the eggs and take DNA samples from the egg-cases to find out how many females were using the area. By diving each month, they confirmed that egg-laying took place in February and March, and that eggs took one and a half years to hatch. Diving in winter is hard work, and when he mentioned that he was looking for help, one of our artists, Rachel Brooks, immediately volunteered, a happy result for everyone.

Because of the flapper skate's large size, they are vulnerable to becoming entangled in scallop dredges or prawn trawls. Parts of the MPA are closed to dredging and prawn-trawling all year, but other parts are closed only in the summer months. The area at the mouth of Loch Sween is bizarrely closed at weekends and after dark. Of course, skate can't read the timetable, so when recently three dead skate were found with thousands of discarded prawns, dumped near Gigha, it was tragic but unsurprising. As they must survive for 10 to 15 years before reproducing, any death will have a massive impact on the population. It's estimated that the adults live for more than 100 years.

As Marnik learned more about the skate, he invited marine scientist James Thorburn and his team from Edinburgh Napier University to use Kilchoan as a base. They have been attaching acoustic tags to flapper skate in the Sound of Jura, and mooring hydrophones that log when a skate passes within 500 metres. It seems that female skate stay in the Sound throughout the year, but males are transient. Tags that record temperature and depth show that in the summer months the skate prefer deeper, colder water, and can dive as deep as 300 metres.

It's so disheartening when an extraordinary animal like the skate is declining right on your doorstep and you can do nothing about it. But rather than become despondent, the community around Loch Craignish, just south of Kilchoan, has decided to look for positive action they can take for their own coastline. There, local Hope Spot group CROMACH has started an amazing initiative called Seawilding. This is the UK's first community-led native oyster and seagrass restoration project. We arranged to take our snorkelling artists there for the day.

Research into local Gaelic placenames reveals that oysters must once have been plentiful in this area. They were a valuable food source, but have been overharvested and now are rare. Oysters provide the sea lochs with valuable 'ecosystem services'. They filter seawater when feeding, and this helps remove sediment so that sunlight can penetrate to the seabed. They also provide a hard substrate on otherwise muddy ground. New oysters cement themselves to living or dead shells, and so build up a reef. Other animals and plants then have a foothold, and a complex community can build up, increasing biodiversity. Oysters also sequester carbon and store it in their shells.

Seawilding plans to release a million oysters into their loch. They have suspended nursery cages full of baby oysters under the pontoons of the village marina. Local school children are involved in the project. They are learning how to grow oysters from tiny shells the size of a fingernail, to a weight of 10 grammes, so they will be less vulnerable to crabs and starfish when they are released into the loch. The children (calling themselves Seawildlings) monitor growth and keep the cages clear of seasquirts which block the vital flow of water. Once released into the wild, the oysters will double in size every year. When they reach a breeding weight of 50 grammes, they will release new spat, so helping to create a self-sustaining population. Their teacher told us how proud the children were that a PhD student was using the data they were collecting in a thesis. I love hearing teachers come up with new ways to connect children with wildlife, and my favourite of the day was the explanation of how much water an adult oyster can filter in one day. 'Two hundred litres is the same as 600 cans of Irn Bru. Even if you sat on the toilet to pee as you drank them, you couldn't drink that much!'

We were invited by Seawilding to snorkel in Loch Craignish to see the seagrass that they are reintroducing, in tandem with the oysters. Seagrass grows in shallow water, which means that it's a colourful snorkelling experience. It provides a

sheltered nursery for silvery shoals of young fish. It feels like being in a woodland, but one where you can fly through the trees amongst great shoals of birds. Brittle-stars brachiate through the foliage like hairy primates, and snakelocks anemones wave their mauve tentacles to gather food. Tiny red urchins climb the grass stalks, and flatfish camouflage themselves against the speckled sand. Seagrass roots grow into a fibrous mat, preventing coastal erosion and creating a stable environment for other animals.

The staff at Seawilding gave us a presentation about their project. They were so enthusiastic about the potential benefits of restoring their coastline. Seagrass plants, like oysters, act as a carbon sink. They take carbon dioxide from the water during photosynthesis and lock it away in the sediment. But 90 per cent of the UK's seagrass has disappeared. Pollution from agricultural run-off, silt from dredging and farmed-fish faeces in the water, block the sunlight that the seagrass meadows need for growth. This is where the oysters come in, filtering the water to let light through.

Seawilding have engaged their whole community to help find the best way of expanding their seagrass meadows. Volunteer snorkellers have been gathering seeds from existing plants and releasing them in trial plots underwater. Some seeds are scattered and some are planted. They have also tried translocating sediment blocks and transplanting rhizomes. The results are monitored by other volunteers on stand-up paddle boards and in kayaks. Because everyone is getting engaged with the underwater world, they have a much greater stake in the health of their coastline. Despite not owning the seabed (which belongs to the Crown) the local community have taken a kind of moral ownership of it. Loch Craignish currently does not have any official protection, but Seawildling are applying to become a Demonstration and Research Marine Protected Area. By sharing their research, they hope to provide a model for how other communities might regenerate their own marine landscapes.

After the 2021 Scottish election, the Scottish National Party negotiated power-sharing with the Green Party, and agreed to consult the public on designating

[opposite] *Seaweed otter*

some areas of the sea as Highly Protected Marine Areas or HPMAs. This would mean no fishing, extraction or deposition of any kind in the area. Fish nurseries would be protected and could then supply and enrich the surrounding waters. In England three HPMAs were designated, but fishing interests there campaigned against them, and plans for Scottish HPMAs were dropped. To survive as a fisherman you need skills of self-reliance and determination. It's a physically demanding job with potential for huge rewards, and nobody wants to give any ground. Fishermen feel that they know the sea better than anyone, and don't want office-based pen-pushers meddling in their affairs. The sea is also a difficult place to police, and this leads to a feeling of mistrust – 'I might agree not to harvest this area, but what's to stop someone else doing it?' is a common response. For now, there is only one 'no-take' zone in Scotland. This is a part of Lamlash Bay on Arran, which is less than three square kilometres. This seems woefully inadequate.

One evening during the snorkelling residency, Dan the Merman offered to host a Gaelic evening. Although he was brought up in London and has a cockney accent when speaking English, his grandparents spoke Irish Gaelic and he is a Scottish Gaelic speaker. His name in Gaelic is Dònal MacGiolla Chomhgaill. He explained how understanding the meaning of placenames can give us a deeper connection with our surroundings. The name Argyll comes from Earra-Ghàidheal which translates as the Coast of the Gaels. Gaelic is spoken in Ireland, the Isle of Man and across Scotland, all communities linked to each other by the sea. He taught us the word Dùthchas, the sense of a deep ancestral belonging to a place, also used for stewardship of the natural world. As Gaelic is most prevalent on the west coast, many of the proverbs are sea-based. 'A' deanamh cuain mhòr de chaolas cumhang' means 'The making of a big ocean out of a narrow strait'. It's equivalent to 'making a mountain out of a molehill', but we decided that instead of being a chastisement it could be used as a positive symbol for the recovery of the sea, working from a small protected area outwards to a healthier ocean.

[opposite] *Eider ducks displaying*

ST KILDA

CHAPTER NINE

SEA

The sea seems such a vast, unknowable place, that when it came to this chapter I struggled with where to start. I got in touch with my friend Ellie Owen, who is now the Senior Seabird Officer for the National Trust for Scotland. She sent me two black-and-white photographs. In the first, a young man is holding a white bird with a sooty black eye. It's a wild fulmar that he is about to release, having put a numbered ring on its leg as part of a scientific study. In the second, an older man with greying hair is holding an identical-looking bird. Both pictures, taken decades apart, are of scientist George Dunnet and 'Bird 57', which lived for over 50 years. Seabirds are long-lived because they need time to build up a knowledge of where to find food in the seemingly featureless landscape. By tracking them on feeding trips and by studying their breeding success, scientists can find out what's going on under the waves. Ellie invited me to join an expedition to Europe's largest seabird colony, the archipelago of St Kilda, to help with a census of the hundreds of thousands of birds that breed there.

The islands lie 100 miles west of mainland Scotland, out towards the edge of the continental shelf. From the hilltops of Harris they are visible as an intriguing smudge on the horizon. Our team of volunteers left Harris at seven in the morning for the three-hour crossing. When you're in a boat, remaining on top of the waves is obviously a good thing, but seeing other creatures pass so easily between the worlds of above and below made the sea seem even more mysterious. Gannets plunge-dived for fish, puffins slid under the surface at our approach, and we had tantalising glimpses of minke whales as they came up to breathe, then vanished under the dancing waves.

My old enemy, seasickness, was getting increasingly hard to hold down, so I was glad when we entered the sheltered bay of the main island, Hirta (Hiort in Gaelic). The islands are the peaks of mountains formed by volcanic activity 60 million years ago. The other islands, Boreray and Soay, are steep-sided and only accessible to the most agile, as are the famous sea-stacks, Stac Li and Stac an Armin. They are covered in breeding ledges with thousands of seabirds. Damp

Swimming puffins

sea air, rising up the cliffs, cools and condenses, and often the islands have clouds shrouding their peaks.

The presence of humans on these islands has always been intertwined with the nesting seabirds. In the past, people harvested the birds to sustain themselves through the long winter. The present-day islanders are studying them to learn more about the health of the sea. Ellie wanted me to write about the community of seabird scientists – those who've inspired her, and also the next generation to whom she's passing on her knowledge. Before we left on the trip, she put me in touch with two men who started the work on St Kilda in the 1970s. Like their subjects, seabird scientists also seem to be long-lived. Mike Harris was in his 80s when I met him doing fieldwork on the sea-cliffs of the Isle of May. He'd been studying puffins there for over 50 years. In 1974 he was sent to St Kilda to find out why puffins were declining. The birds did subsequently recover, and this grew his confidence in them. 'Seabirds can look after themselves, as long as we don't mess up their environment,' he told me.

I also visited his work partner, Stuart Murray, in Edinburgh. Having had a stroke, Stuart is now restricted to a wheelchair, but is famous for having climbed every stack on St Kilda bar one. 'I'm happy to call myself a birdwatcher,' he told me, 'although nowadays it's more pigeons and woodpeckers that get my interest.' He and Mike worked together. 'Mike's a grafter. You'd have to go some to beat his enthusiasm for fieldwork. Puffin-work was hard. There were 200 study burrows. You'd be covered in crap and bitten 'til you needed a blood transfusion!' But studying puffins was not always tough. When the chicks were ready to leave their burrows on Hirta under cover of darkness, they would sometimes get distracted by the lights of the island's army base. Pufflings are cute, with soft bills, and the scientists would collect them up to release them safely elsewhere. Stuart remembered that they also seemed to like the vibration of the generator. 'You'd go out at night and find half a dozen of them standing there worshipping it.'

Most of their work was on the island of Dun on the far side of Village Bay. Until medieval times it was part of Hirta, but a big storm broke through the cliffs, and now the island is ungrazed and full of puffin burrows.

The sea channel is narrow, and Stuart set up a breeches buoy to avoid the dangerous daily landing on the exposed rocky shore. Suspended in the breeches (trousers) and life-buoy, they would haul each other across the narrow gap. The buoy lasted four summers before finally succumbing to the salt spray and corrosion.

Ellie told me she was envious of Mike and Stuart's research back then. No-one knew how many puffins there were, or anything much of their basic natural history, and they discovered so much.

'Most people don't get to meet their heroes,' she said, 'but I can phone them up. I'll tell them "I've thought of this solution" and they say "Oh yes, we did that 50 years ago, but we just used a bit of baler twine." ' She's joking of course, but also adds that when she writes up her work, 'they will push me to make it as good as it possibly can be'.

There are still many unknowns, and Ellie can build on their research and that of others, using new technology as it becomes available. When I first met her on Colonsay in 2011, she was using GPS trackers attached to large seabirds like fulmars, to find out where they were feeding when raising chicks. Catching the birds involved techniques developed by the original St Kildans, who would lower themselves down the cliffs to capture seabirds using a noose on a pole. Ellie had the much more difficult task of catching each bird a second time, to retrieve the tracker with its precious information. She enjoyed the fieldcraft of causing minimum stress and spending time making sure the individual settled down post-capture. The data would only be valid if the bird continued its normal routine.

The second time we worked together was to study puffins breeding in Shetland in 2016. By then the data from the birds could be transmitted via a UHF radio link to a base station set up at the edge of the colony, and the tag would fall off after a few days, so the bird need only be caught once. By 2023, GPS tags were now so tiny that they could be put on birds as small as warblers.

Warblers only live a few years, so they have simple survival strategies. Their feeding area when nesting may be only 100 metres across, and if they find a successful overwintering location, they automatically return there every year. Small animals with faster heartrates tend to live less long, but seabirds push the boundaries, some of them living nearly as long as us. Human adolescence is spent in learning the best places to find food, so by the time we have children we know how to feed not only ourselves but them as well. I have a friend who has to visit every café in a street before she decides which one to buy coffee in. In that case, choice is a luxury (or maybe a handicap), but we all have our favourite supermarket that suits our budget. Not only do seabirds need to discover the food-rich areas where undersea ridges push nutrient-rich water to the surface, but they need to be able to return to them again. They may fly hundreds of miles to gather food for their chick. A good memory and a long life suggest sentience, which is what I recognise when a fulmar flies past me on a clifftop, gliding in close to check me out.

If a fulmar can survive to seven years old, then it knows enough to start breeding. It will need a cliff with many sheltered ledges flat enough to lay an egg. It prefers to breed near other fulmars for protection in numbers, but unlike guillemots which crowd together, fulmar couples like their own space. As their wings are designed for long-distance gliding rather than flapping, they like a high, steep rockface where they can launch straight into an up-draft. The geology of St Kilda is perfect. It has the tallest sea-cliff in the British Isles, 430 metres high. Its granite rock, which is softer than the Lewisian gneiss of the nearby Outer Hebrides, fractures into perfect ledges. What's more, being so far out to the west, near the upwellings of the continental shelf, it's close to a reliable food supply. No wonder St Kilda is home to the biggest fulmar colony in Europe.

There's another reason why islands are good for ground-nesters like fulmars. When we arrived in Village Bay, we were instructed on the VHF radio to approach the jetty in an open boat. St Kildans have always been vulnerable to invaders, whether Vikings or rival clans, but today it's not people that pose the biggest threat, but rats. Amazingly these predators have never arrived on the archipelago, and the National Trust for Scotland (NTS) who manage the islands, are keen to keep it that way. The islands host a small military base and radar station, and this can mean deliveries of bulky equipment. The supply ship runs up onto the sand of the beach and lets down a ramp from the bows. NTS staff mount biosecurity surveillance. If any rats left the ship an 'incursion response' would be triggered, with bait traps placed all around the bay. Chocolate-flavoured wax blocks are used regularly to monitor for rat-sized teeth-marks, but so far only the endemic St Kilda field mice have been snacking on them.

The main reason our team had come to St Kilda was to make a count of the cliff-nesting seabirds. Half of the birds on the island breed underground; burrow-nesting puffins, Leach's petrels, European storm petrels and Manx shearwaters need different census techniques from the cliff-nesters, but even without this, we were daunted by the scale of our task. We examined maps and photographs, and tried to divide the coast into manageable chunks. For fulmars we needed to count 'Apparently Occupied Nests' or AONs. As it was June, one member of each pair should be sitting tight, incubating a single egg, so we could ignore all moving birds.

The count takes place every ten years to compare the population size over time. It has to be standardised and consistent, or we would just be comparing how well different people count seabirds. We spent a day practising together to get within 10 per cent of each other. As is well known from a certain TV baking show, it's always bad to be in the bottom two, especially if you have a soggy bottom, which is common when sitting on a seabird cliff. Counting had to take place between 8am and 5pm. Birds have daily routines. Guillemots' numbers fluctuate, as they usually fit in a final feeding session at the end of the day. This is lucky, because we needed to go back to base and do the same.

It was hard going, climbing the steep hills carrying tripod, telescope, binoculars and packed lunch, but worth it to be able to sit and watch the cliffs. Some were like the hanging gardens of Babylon, with verdant guano-nourished vegetation cascading down from rocky balconies, each one with a white fulmar sitting there watching their circling neighbours. Every so often a sea eagle would fly along the cliff, hoping to grab an unsuspecting meal. All the non-incubators would take wing, floating sunlit against the shadowed wall as if someone had shaken out a feather pillow. Sea eagles have only recently returned to St Kilda, which worries Ellie. In their nests in the Outer Isles, the remains of up to 70 fulmars per year have been found.

One hundred years ago, when St Kildans harvested the cliffs, they also favoured fulmars, especially the young, fat chicks just before fledging. Figures from the 1830s show they were taking at least 20,000 a year to see them through the winter months. It must have been smelly as well as dangerous work, as the fulmars defend themselves by projectile-vomiting a fishy oil. This gave them their name of 'foul mar' or smelly gull, not complimentary for such a beautiful bird. Their carcasses were hung inside stone cleitean (small buildings) to dry in the wind, and there are more than 1,500 of these rock shelters still dotted all over the island.

Until 1930 this was the only place they nested in Britain. When people left the island, bird numbers increased and in less than 100 years they spread as far as the south coast of England. As Ellie says, St Kilda is, quite literally, the fulmar motherland. I was fascinated to find out what our counts would reveal about their current situation.

Unlike fulmars, gannets seem to prefer nesting in a packed and noisy crowd. Ellie had booked a boat to take us around the uninhabited island of Boreray and its sea-stacks. Until recently, before it was overtaken by the Bass Rock in the North Sea, it held the world's largest gannet colony – a quarter of the world's population. Stuart described it as 'astonishingly good fun, so noisy and aggressive, full of vim and vigour'. He told me how difficult it was to land there. 'I slipped into the sea

[opposite] *Fulmars*

once – and I didn't like it.' He got washed off Stac an Armin, but fortunately the next wave washed him back on.

In 1985 he and his colleagues attempted to count the breeding gannets, and the survey has been repeated every ten years since. We had brought a drone to take photos of the nesting gannets so they could be counted later with the aid of computerised dot-counting. This avoided the perilous landing, and reduced disturbance, but like many of our technological advances, it reduced direct contact with the wildlife. It was still a memorable experience touring the sea-stacks by boat. The dark, bird-circled spires soared above us, and nesting gannets crowded onto every available flat space. Since the annual harvest stopped in 1930, their numbers have increased. Of all seabirds, gannets are the most adaptable, as their 2-metre wingspan allows them to fly huge distances. They plunge dive, so can feed in many different layers of the sea, swallowing anything from small sprats to large mackerel.

High on Stac an Armin, the UK's tallest sea-stack, we could see the bothy where the St Kildans lived on their hunting trips. It was more like a pile of stones, perched on the precipitous rock. I couldn't imagine even reaching that place, let alone sleeping there. Every year a group of men and boys lived on the rock for several weeks to harvest several thousand gannets. The islanders traditionally weren't fishermen, partly because the surrounding sea is so exposed and dangerous, but also because they didn't need to be. The seabirds did the job of harvesting fish from far and wide to grow a fat chick, and the people ate the birds. Every decade there would be a death as someone fell from the cliffs, but that was less risky than a whole boatload of men being lost at sea.

The gannets may have been released from human persecution, but as I watched the birds returning to the colony from fishing trips, I realised that another predator had moved in at the top of the food chain. The dark silhouettes of great skuas accelerated towards any gannet arriving with fish. An exhilarating chase would ensue, the quarry jinking and diving, the pursuer catching at tail or wing feathers to tumble the gannet until it disgorged the food. The skua swooped to catch the fish before it reached the sea. The scientific word for this is kleptoparasitism, but

[opposite] *Gannets, courtship display*

basically, it's piracy. Rather than fish for themselves, the skuas let the gannets do the long-distance flying and deep diving, then use their superior bulk and speed to steal the bounty.

Because the skuas are at the top of the food pyramid, there are only a few hundred breeding in the archipelago, and globally they are rare. They nest on the clifftops and defend their territories vigorously. This was a problem when we were counting seabirds. Most gave good warning of an attack, calling raucously before dive-bombing us with a swooping whoosh of feathers, but others approached at eye-level with determination, and we'd have to duck or be knocked on the head. I started carrying the tripod extended above me to protect myself from the aerial bombardment. In Shetland great skuas are called by their Norse name of bonxie, and this name is now used widely, maybe because it well-describes a bird that bonks you on the head.

Not only do different seabirds specialise in hunting techniques that suit their abilities and body design, but there is also specialisation within species. If one food source dries up for a year, then at least some of the population will survive. Some of the great skuas on St Kilda feed at night, predating Leach's petrels, which return to their burrows under cover of darkness. Numbers of these small petrels are declining on the archipelago, and so scientific attention is turning to the skuas to determine if they are to blame.

Derren Fox is working on this for the RSPB. Ellie introduces me with the words, 'This is Jane. I think you've slept with her husband,' – actually true, as Mark shared a room with Derren in South Georgia, when he was there filming albatrosses. On St Kilda, Derren's first task is to dissect skua pellets. These regurgitated, undigestible remains of the skua's prey, mainly skulls and feathers, will show what they have been eating.

St Kilda is home to 80 per cent of the European population of Leach's petrels. These dainty seabirds are rarely seen, as they spend most of their life at sea. They feed in the top few centimetres of the ocean, dancing on the water to pick food off the surface. This makes them dependent on ocean upwellings, and all their breeding colonies are within 70 kilometres of the Atlantic continental shelf.

Ellie and Derren invite me to accompany them on an adventure, to see if the petrels have returned. We leave in the evening for a two-hour scramble, 1,000 feet up to the clifftop, back down a steep slope to the sea and then up through a boulder-field. Puffins take off and wheel overhead. We arrive on our ledge by 11pm as the sun is setting. From this height the sea is laid out like a vast plain stretching to the distant horizon. We drink hot chocolate and try to be patient. I ask Ellie why she has dedicated her working life to seabirds. 'I think I'm a problem-solver, and seabirds are in decline,' she says. 'We've got so much to learn. How many are there, where do they feed in summer, where do they go in winter?' Derren will spend the summer fitting tiny trackers to the petrels to answer some of these questions.

By 1am it's almost dark. We can see a few stars in the clear sky. We're beginning to think the birds won't arrive, when we hear a distant squeaky call, like a fairy having a tantrum. Ellie passes me the thermal binoculars. Below, I can see tiny silhouettes like swallows, flittering above the slope. Gradually, numbers build until we are pressing ourselves against the hillside out of their way, feeling the air from their wings on our faces. An orange moon rises above us and Ellie turns to me. 'This is why,' she whispers. We put our ears to the ground and can hear the soft churring of petrels talking to each other in their burrows. It's magical.

The night quietens, but we can't leave until we can see where we're putting our feet. We all curl up together as it's surprisingly cold, but it's not easy to sleep on a grassy slope with a huge drop to the sea below. At 4am seals start singing in the sea caves and there's enough light to move. We can see pale feathers caught on the grass – evidence that the bonxies were out last night too.

By the time we reach the clifftop, our muscles have warmed up. In the half-light it feels like we are closer to the people who lived here 100 years ago. We pass many of their tiny stone buildings. Their name, cleit, is from the Norse *klettr*, for rock, which suggests that they were used a 1,000 years ago in Viking times. They were built to store food and fuel, both being vital for the human community to survive the winter here. Meat and cut peats were sheltered from the rain and dried by the wind that whistled through the gaps left in the stonework. In Village Bay the cleitean are tall enough to stand up in, but here on the cliffs they are long and low, like stone bivy bags. Some are built right out on a rock spur, as if their maker was showing off.

The sun is starting to rise as we descend the mountain above Village Bay. The ruins of the blackhouses, field-walls and croft houses are laid out in a fan below us. Because no trees grew on the island, people built everything using the rocks which tumble from screes on the high peaks. These granite boulders have a rough surface texture, which grips well without mortar. They are heavy, so are never carried very far. Stones used as field hoes in Neolithic times are reused in cleitean thousands of years later, and these still stand today. The history of human occupation is written on the land.

People survived because of their strong community organisation. One of the most famous photos of St Kildans is of the daily meeting of the village parliament, when jobs for the day were shared out. Barefooted, bearded men gather on the narrow cobbled track with their dogs. The cliffs were divided up among the crofts for harvesting, and rotated each year. In the late 1800s there were 16 shares, one for each house. A share was 80 young gannets, 120 adult gannets, 560 fulmars, 600 puffins, 120 guillemots and 50 razorbills. Seabirds were caught by the young men who were lowered over the cliffs on long ropes. Ellie showed me the Mistress Stone, a massive boulder wedged at an angle into the sea-cliff. The men stood on the boulder on one leg to prove that they were marriage material; agile and daring enough to support a family.

Some birds were exported to pay rent to the laird, and some were salted for food in winter. The feathers were sold to make feather beds. In winter, islanders lived off beef and lamb, cheese, fish, salted seabirds and their eggs, barley, oats, potatoes, seaweed and wild sorrel. But like the seabirds, towards the end of winter they would lose weight. They survived on rehydrated, salted fulmar, and when tobacco ran out, they would smoke moss. Farming was hard work; the fields were fertilised with animal dung, seaweed, peat and the remnants of the seabird harvest.

The island population was vulnerable. In 1727 a smallpox epidemic killed all but one adult and 18 children on Hirta. Three more men and eight boys survived because they were away hunting on Stac an Armin. No-one was left alive who could use the boat to fetch them, and they lived on the rock for nine months over

[opposite] *St Kilda sheep*

the winter before they were rescued. The island was then repopulated by people from Skye and Harris. In 1852, 36 islanders emigrated to Australia, reducing the population to 74. In September 1885 a storm swept away the corn and barley, and the islanders sent out the 'St Kilda mailboat'. This was a carved block of hollowed wood containing a plea for help, which washed up on a beach in Lewis.

The population remained low, as many newborn children died of infantile tetanus. Traditionally the cut umbilical cord was smeared with fulmar oil stored in a gannet's stomach, which may well have fostered the tetanus bacteria. For some families, only one child out of nine births might survive. Whilst younger people did the heavy labour of bird-catching or farming, their elders wove tweed. At the beginning of the 1900s, high demand for St Kilda cloth allowed the aging population to continue living there. However, when World War One broke out, demand switched to khaki cloth, and tourist boats stopped visiting. By 1928 numbers had dropped to 37 people, with only seven able-bodied men who could harvest the birds. In 1930 the remaining islanders decided to leave. This exodus has been mythologised by many people over the years, all using it as evidence against whatever 'ism' they dislike: capitalism, modernism, feudalism, religion. My own conclusion is that the island wasn't repopulated as it had been before, because its products no longer had value. Fulmar oil had been replaced by fossil fuels. Duvets could be filled with polyester instead of feathers. Factory-farmed chicken could provide cheaper eggs.

Gannet populations also live in a few offshore colonies, and are vulnerable to food shortages and to disease in the same way as the St Kildans. When bird flu swept across Scotland in 2022, it spread quickly through the tightly packed gannet colonies and thousands died. Widowed birds toured other colonies and spread the virus. Bird flu seems to be waterborne, and bonxies, which gather for communal bathing sessions in freshwater lochs, lost two-thirds of their population on St Kilda.

The reason seabirds are usually long-lived is because life at sea is so unpredictable. In some years fish are plentiful and chicks can be raised successfully. In other years storms or disease wreak havoc and no chicks fledge. Predator numbers fluctuate too – the Leach's petrels will have easier years until bonxie numbers recover. Added to natural pressures are those caused by humans: competition from commercial fisheries, entanglement in nets, predation from rats, consumption of plastics, disturbance from offshore wind farms, and the changing of ocean currents by global warming.

The results of our St Kilda seabird count were shocking. Since the last count in 1999, the numbers of nesting fulmars were down by 69 per cent, razorbills and guillemots by 35 per cent and kittiwakes were down by 84 per cent. It's a clear sign that the marine ecosystem is under immense pressure. St Kilda has already been witness to the extinction of one seabird. In 1840 some St Kilda men camping on Stac an Armin, captured a great auk. It was the last individual ever recorded in the British Isles. They imprisoned the auk, but when an unseasonal storm blew up, they suspected the bird of being a witch, so they beat it to death.

'Seabirds have been declining my whole career,' Ellie tells me. But faith in humanity is what keeps her going. She believes that if she can gather the data to show what's happening, people will make the right decisions. And a few months after our return from the island, Ellie posted a message on our St Kilda WhatsApp group. 'Have you guys seen the amazing news today? Sandeel fishing permanently banned in English North Sea and all Scottish waters :). This has been some people's life's work but we are very lucky to see it happen in our lifetime. Come on the seabirds!!!!'.

And what of the future of St Kilda? Now that nature and wilderness have become so depleted, the islands hold a resource that has value. Society is once again happy to maintain a community there, but now catching seabirds for a very different reason.

GLASGOW

CHAPTER TEN

CITY

Arriving in Glasgow by train from the south, I pass through a farmland of huge rolling green fields. This is our countryside, but the only plant growing here is ryegrass, and the only birds seem to be magpies. We cross the River Clyde with a few loitering gulls, and enter a bustling Central Station, busy not only with people but also city pigeons. They're a hardy breed, descended from wild rock doves and interbred with our domestic pigeons. They're used to surviving on whatever is available, but can other wildlife survive in our urban jungle?

I catch a bus to my daughter's flat, and walk the last leg through the park. At the pond, children are feeding the ducks. Mute swans swim past and moorhens creep between the iris flags. I looked up the species list for Queen's Park on eBird; more than 60 bird species have been logged here. The flat is on the top floor, looking out over a bit of rough ground with trees. Jackdaws are gathering twigs to build a nest under the eaves of a neighbour's house. Pink bullfinches are feeding on fresh new buds and a wren is singing loudly from the undergrowth. On the grass below, a fox is basking in the sun. Wildlife has to adapt to the landscapes we make, and in the city there is a wider diversity of habitats than in some parts of the countryside.

Glasgow is my local city. Despite it being a three-hour drive away, I feel a sense of belonging, and also pride in its energy and diversity. Who wouldn't love a place where you can choose between Vietnamese street food, pizza, Sichuan dumplings or pad Thai noodles? The city hosted the COP 26 Climate Change Conference, and people are aware of their environmental responsibilities. There's now even a music venue, SWG3, which is striving for net zero by using the energy generated by the dancing clubbers to heat or cool the building. But on this trip I have come to visit one of the city's older establishments. I've arranged to meet John Simpson outside the Hogwarts-style main building of Glasgow University. I find him easily as he's carrying binoculars and a telescope – incongruous in the city, but he'll need them to show me the peregrines that are nesting in the university's iconic Gilbert Scott Tower.

A few years ago, John volunteered to be the Clyde Area Bird Recorder for the Scottish Ornithologists' Club (SOC). He's also involved with his local Raptor

Study Group, and was looking for a project where he could use his knowledge to make a positive difference for wildlife. He'd been monitoring peregrine breeding sites outside the city around Loch Lomond, and in 2022, for the first time, there were no birds nesting. Wading bird populations and gull colonies had declined in the hills, pigeon-racing was less of a hobby, and so peregrines were struggling to find food. Those that could breed were having their chicks stolen by thieves. A single chick can be sold for £10,000 to the falconry trade. When peregrines started breeding in the city again after years of absence, it seemed like a great opportunity to share their story with a wider audience.

We set up the telescope near the university library, and quickly spot the male peregrine sitting on the spire. This round tower provides a sheltered side in any wind, and the ornate decoration gives plenty of perches. From this height he can wait until he sees a pigeon or a gull flying at an ideal speed and direction. He slips off the building and stoops down on his prey, smacking into it with his sharp talons. Peregrines are the fastest travelling animals in the world, and can dive at more than 200mph. He plucks the prey and brings it to his mate, who is incubating their eggs on a balcony of the tower.

The female is called L7, the number written on her leg-ring. She received this as a chick at Norwich Cathedral in 2019, before travelling 350 miles north to set up her own territory here. She was an inexperienced parent in 2021 when she laid eggs in a gutter on the roof of Glasgow Cathedral. They got flooded when it rained, so the pair moved location and evicted nesting ravens from the Gilbert Scott Tower. They successfully fledged three chicks in 2022 and 2023, and this year are incubating four eggs. It's not known where the male fledged from, but feather detail on his head suggests that one of his ancestors may have been an escaped falconry bird like a lanner falcon. He can often be seen perching on the tower below a stone gothic falcon.

Through the SOC, John set up the Glasgow Peregrine Project with the aim of bringing together local and national wildlife groups to collaborate for the good of the peregrines. The University Geography Department has offered help with data

[opposite] *Peregrine*

mapping, and the Scottish Government Species Champion for peregrines, MSP Bob Doris, has visited the site. John is trying to run the scheme at minimal cost, to show that it could be reproduced in other cities.

As we stand next to the telescope, chatting, students are emerging from the library for a study break. They ask to look through the scope, and are captivated. One student, studying genetics, is reminded how much she loved fieldwork. Another said the experience of the natural world was a welcome relief from the stress of exams. John shows them a live feed on his phone from cameras looking directly into the nest, and invites them to return the following Saturday, when local wildlife groups will be running a 'peregrine watch' event. These popular free events will run every weekend until the birds fledge in late June. They attract hundreds of people from Glasgow and visitors from all over the world.

A criticism often aimed at voluntary projects is that they run out of steam once the original instigator steps down, and so John is delighted to engage with the students. 'In the past,' he tells me, 'Raptor Study Groups have been run like a gentleman's club. Raptor enthusiasts tend to be male, and they can be quite territorial.' But now young people (of both sexes) are getting involved in the project, and everyone benefits. 'They are younger and fitter than us, with a better understanding of the technology available, and we can offer them the practical experience of fieldwork that they need. When we started out, all we had was an interest, but now these students have careers ahead of them. Most modern developments nowadays need environmental impact assessments.' John has offered study projects to students and young birders in the city. If they can log where the birds are hunting and what they are eating, it will provide data on what the birds need for successful breeding.

When the chicks can control their own body temperature and are large enough to defend themselves, the female can leave them. She too must hunt to provide enough food for the growing brood, although in the city she doesn't need to travel far.

The peregrines have cleverly chosen an inaccessible nest site where they are safe from falconry thieves, but this gives John a problem. To study them, the chicks need to be marked with individual rings. John's colleague, George Smith, also wants to take DNA swabs to build a database of all wild Scottish peregrines. This helps ascertain whether birds, claimed to be captive-bred, have been stolen from the wild. This information has already helped catch criminals responsible for the failure of many Scottish nests. There is a window of opportunity to do this work when the chicks are three weeks old; they're big enough to fit a ring on their leg, but not so well-grown that they might try to leave the nest if disturbed. The clock is ticking. John has to find people qualified to handle these birds who also have the ropework certification to satisfy the university. Climbers need to abseil down the tower to the nest and bring the chicks back up to the ringers. To fix anchors to the historic masonry requires someone with 2,000 hours of relevant experience (and therefore a very expensive day-rate). All the publicity around the project only increases the pressure.

On the big day, experts arrive from as far as Bristol to help with the well-planned operation. Access to the spire starts with a dizzying climb up a tiny spiral stone staircase. From the top there's a phenomenal view over Glasgow. 'The peregrines have the best penthouse address in the city,' says John. Standing on the parapet the climbers check their ropes and harnesses. They will collect the four chicks in individual pillowcases to keep them calm.

Once the chicks are brought up, the team must work fast to minimise disruption. But care is needed too. Peregrine chicks have huge feet, with talons strong enough to draw blood if not handled carefully. Measuring their feet reveals their sex – three males and one female – with the female's feet being larger (as a woman with size 44 feet, I'm pleased by that). The chicks are covered in white down with their flight feathers just starting to appear. They are weighed, and marked in three ways – a unique metal British Trust for Ornithology ring, a Raptor Study Group colour ring with large numbers which can be read from a distance and, incorporated into this, a microchip PIT tag. This can save information about where the bird has been, which can be downloaded to a receiver at the nest.

The day has been a success. The PIT tags will provide much-needed information on juvenile dispersal, and all the SOC data will be made available for use by students. As the chicks are returned to the nest, the adults scream around the tower, hoping to intimidate the intruders. They make so much noise, the university security team come into the quadrangle to see what the matter is. In a few weeks, when the

chicks fledge, their help will be vital. Every year at least one of the chicks ends up in the courtyards and the staff will have to put them somewhere safe where the adults can feed them until they are ready to fly with confidence.

'The peregrines have become standard-bearers for wildlife in Glasgow,' John tells me. He's hoping that the Glasgow Peregrine Project (GPP) can collaborate with the City Council to create a walking trail, connecting them with the other nesting birds of prey: kestrels on the Finnieston crane, sparrowhawks and ravens at Anniesland gasometer. These city birds are all nesting in post-industrial sites and predating mice and rats.

The GPP is not the only community wildlife regeneration project springing up in Glasgow. I meet my next interviewee, Dr Hilary Wilson, when she visits my Open Studio and tells me how she'd been inspired into action at the Glasgow Royal Infirmary. Hilary works at the hospital as a consultant rheumatologist, and during Covid she realised how uninviting the hospital was looking. 'There was nothing growing in the flower tubs at the entrance, just cigarette butts.' No-one else was fixing the problem, so she bought some flowers and planted them herself. This gesture, in theory quite simple, rippled outwards in its effects. She was joined by consultant nephrologist Dr Kate Stevens and together they set about improving the hospital grounds. A hospital is such a huge and multifaceted community that making change might seem a daunting task, but Hilary and Kate use that to their advantage. 'We're waiting for the bubble to burst, but no-one's stopped us yet. We just crack on and ask for forgiveness later,' Kate told me. With advice from Glasgow Botanic Gardens and sponsorship from local companies, they planted a biodiversity garden which benefits both wildlife and people. Staff can take a break from a stressful day to eat their lunch outside in relaxing surroundings.

They kept going, and planted a medicinal garden, an orchard and now have their sights set on the cemetery next to the hospital, 'The New Burial Ground'. It's a rare green space in the area, and offers an opportunity to learn about the city's fascinating history and its nature. They also want to communicate the importance of being physically active, not because the occupants of the burial ground are

[opposite] *Lesser black-backed gulls*

no longer so, but because there is so much benefit in 'just moving'. A short walk around the graveyard will enable a reset and improve wellbeing.

Hilary and Kate also decided to get the hospital its own beehives. In medicine there's been a long association with honey, because of its antibiotic properties. Beekeeping is also a great way to learn about the natural world. Although honey bees are a domesticated species, if beekeeping inspires people to plant more bee-friendly flowers, then this can also have a positive effect on native insects like bumblebees. The bees have encouraged a sense of community at the hospital. Different departments have sponsored a beehive, with everyone competing to come up with the best team name. Bee-tablocker was popular in the cardiology department, and endosco-bee with the surgical team. Managing a hive must be very like diagnosing patients. A lot of it is experience and watching for patterns of behaviour. Not an exact science, more of a behavioural science. You have to check the bees regularly to make sure they are healthy, and to prevent a swarm. Hilary and Kate have learned about all this from local beekeeper Mike Duncan, and he kindly allowed me to join him when inspecting the hives.

Mike arrives at the hospital on his bicycle, which has a homemade trailer to carry spare frames for the hives. He has brought a white jacket with a hood which he zips me into. He lights newspaper and cardboard in a tin with a bellows, which he uses to puff smoke over the hive to calm the bees. As he opens the lid the buzzing sound increases and bees start knocking into us as a warning – a bit like head-butting (which is known popularly here as a Glasgow kiss). Stinging is a last resort, but the bees are definitely trying to discourage us. I can't tell if the bees in front of my face are inside or outside of the hood mesh, but I force myself to be calm and concentrate on what Mike is telling me. I'm amazed how most of them stay clustered on the frames as he lifts them out.

The bees have built beautiful wax hexagonal cells on the frames. Mike's relieved to see grubs curled up inside them: new workers for the year ahead. They are females which are unable to reproduce, but instead will do all the work of the colony. They are being fed by their overwintered sisters, who will soon die. Larger cells contain grubs of the unfertilised male drones. Their only job is to mate with

[opposite] *Beekeeping*

a new queen. Every few years the workers somehow decide collectively that the queen is past her prime and must be deposed. They sneakily build a drone cell, but once the queen has laid an egg there, they will enlarge it and keep feeding royal jelly to the grub. Mike must watch out for these larger cells, as eight days after the new queen hatches, the old queen will leave. She will take half the colony with her as a swarm, so before this happens, he must remove her and settle her into a new hive with some of her retinue.

The new queen will fly on warm days to mate with drones from her own and other hives. She may receive sperm from up to 12 males, which she will use for the next few years. Mike will put 'supers' above the hive to hold frames, screened with mesh to prevent the queen from egg-laying in them. This is where the workers will store the honey. In Spring this will be nectar from tree blossom, then, later on, wild flowers will provide a different flavour of honey. As Mike points out, the affectionate nickname of Glasgow is the 'Dear Green Place'. It's from the Gaelic name of the city, 'Glas Chu'. Glas can be translated either as green or grey. (As an artist I am obsessed with the subtleties of colour, and a greeny-grey is much more interesting than the pure colour.)

At Christmas the two doctors sell the honey from their bees to support their projects. I ask Hilary and Kate, both respected and hardworking consultants, why they have taken on these extra projects when they must be so busy already. 'Because it's fun,' they say. 'Initially people said, "What are those two up to now?" They thought we were a bit mad, but now people get behind us and believe in what we're doing, and that makes us believe in it too.'

I want to find out whether there are enough flowering plants in the city to sustain the bees and other pollinators. I get in touch with Glasgow City Council, and arrange to meet their Biodiversity Officer, Cath Scott in Hogganfield Park. I have to wait until she returns from her holiday in Düsseldorf where she went to see her favourite German heavy metal band. I can tell from our emails that we're going to get along. Cath has been working for the Council for 24 years, and is super-enthusiastic with a contagious laugh.

Hogganfield is on the eastern edge of Glasgow. The park surrounds a loch that used to have concrete edges. Cath has worked with the Seven Lochs Wetland Park and volunteer groups to plant wild flowers like meadowsweet and irises, and build floating islands. All the extra vegetation takes up nutrients which helps prevent algal blooms. Cath has also been experimenting to find the best way of growing wildflower meadows. The most efficient way is to remove the top layer of turf, but this is expensive. Scarifying the ground before sowing seed seems to work well. She proudly shows me a field full of bird's-foot trefoil, ox-eye daisies and cuckoo flowers (good for orange-tip butterflies). Orchids are exciting because they just appear when and where they want to; in the middle of the field is a beautiful white greater butterfly orchid.

But there's a special reason why Cath has become obsessed with grasslands. In 2008 environmental health officers were called out to a reported rat infestation in grassland in the east end of the city. They found animals slightly smaller than rats, with round faces and shortish tails. Could they be water voles? These rare animals make their burrows in river banks and are endangered in the UK. Cath went out to take a look. 'We couldn't believe it, because there was no water nearby. We called NatureScot to confirm we weren't losing the plot.'

What were the voles doing here? A hundred years ago this was grazed farmland – no good for voles, which prefer long grass. In the 1950s the Council built new housing schemes like Easterhouse on the city outskirts. They relocated people from the slums of Glasgow, overcrowded with workers who had flocked to the city to work in the shipyards. The nearby Monklands Canal, which used to bring coal into the city from the Central Belt, was filled in and converted into the M8 motorway. It's thought that water voles living on the canal banks were also forced to move, and now the relocated communities of voles and people live side-by-side. 'We started looking around and kept finding more and more,' Cath told me. Although water voles can swim, they don't have webbed feet or similar adaptations for an aquatic life. Swimming allows them to escape land predators, but puts them in danger from aquatic predators like mink and otters. Water voles living on river banks are the same species as the 'fossorial' water voles living in parks, the only difference is behavioural. Instead of asking 'Why do water voles live in grasslands?' should the question be 'Why do they live on waterways?' I wonder if it's because in farmland, the only rough grassland left is along drainage ditches.

Cath takes me to a suburban park with tennis courts, a playground and dog-walkers. We search in the long grass next to the bowling club, and quickly find signs of water voles. There are many large burrow entrances, 8 centimetres across, with piles of excavated soil like molehills. The females dig the burrows, with chambers for food storage and for breeding. They mark their territory with latrines (piles of poo). Cath tells me what to look for. Whereas bank and field voles have poo the size of rice grains, she describes water vole droppings as looking like brown Tic Tacs. She eventually finds some. 'There's your Tic Tacs. I wouldn't eat them though.' We find a dead vole and it's surprisingly big, the size of a guinea pig with a soft silky black coat. I ask Cath if she ever sees live ones. 'Not often. You have to sit very still and I'm always on the go.'

The voles eat grass, their favourite being Yorkshire fog. In winter when the vegetation dies down, they live mostly underground and survive on plant roots and stored food. Snow allows them to get out and about safely underneath the surface crust. The voles seem to do better where there are more humans. Maybe the disturbance keeps predators like herons, foxes and gulls away.

Because water voles are so rare, Glasgow University came on board to survey them. 'It was a steep learning curve,' says Cath. Traps were baited with apple and the voles were microchipped (like pet cats). Some were even given mini radio-collars to gauge the extent of their home range. Their burrows, which can be a metre deep, were mapped with ground penetrating radar. Predictive mapping was used to show where new populations might be.

Cath drives me all around the east end of the city. We stop outside the Easterhouse swimming baths. 'This is the closest the voles get to water here,' she laughs. We stop to have lunch with a group from the Conservation Volunteers. They are tidying up some abandoned land on what used to be a primary school. Walking across the former playground, I can just see the netball-court markings between the trees that have pushed through the tarmac. This is near the Ruchazie scheme where the infamous ice-cream-van drug wars took place, and the area has a very low score on the Scottish Index of Multiple Deprivation. Claire and Harley run the volunteer

[opposite] *Water vole*

Bus Stop
19

group and are extremely knowledgeable and positive about urban wildlife. 'Where there is fly-tipping there is an opportunity,' jokes Harley. He points out a pile of old rubble which they will cover in sand for solitary bees to nest in. 'The bees will provide ecosystem services as pollinators for the community garden.' The volunteers have a wide variety of backgrounds and needs, and all support each other in a really heartwarming way. People are gaining living skills, employability skills, learning how to use tools and machinery. Others gain training to go and do wildlife surveys. Tom, who is retired, likes to keep active and help others. Mark says, 'It gets me out of the house to meet people.' 'The voles give the community around here something to be proud of,' says Cath.

Water voles seem happy to move into vacant, derelict land, as long there is long grass. There are folk who feel that mown grass is neater, and the Council website gets complaints, but Cath is trying to convert people. I'm starting to see the urban landscape through her eyes. She's always on the lookout for land that she can annex for wildlife – a motorway verge, a roadside embankment or vacant plot. She needs space to relocate vole refugees when their homes are being developed for new housing. But she still can't predict them. At one site she had a beautiful marshy area created for them, but they preferred the dug-out spoil heap next to it.

The water voles have now become a focus for bigger conservation projects. Cath works with the Glasgow Clyde Valley Green Network, who are linking up green spaces like the Seven Lochs Wetland Park, so that the communities of both wildlife and people can move around the city using a network of green paths.

[opposite] *Great crested grebe and meadowsweet*

ISLE OF EIGG

CHAPTER ELEVEN

COMMUNITY

In 2022 the Isle of Eigg, in the Inner Hebrides, celebrated 25 years of community ownership. Whereas the island of St Kilda is famous for the death of its community, Eigg is known for its rebirth, and it has inspired hundreds of other community buyouts. Mark and I visited the island for the anniversary and attended a talk by Maggie Fyffe, who was instrumental in achieving the purchase in 1997. She said the transition was 'very, very hard won'. Unlike today, there was no Scottish government funding to support community land purchases. She told us that they wouldn't have attempted the project if they hadn't been so desperate. Back then, only 68 people were left on the island, which was managed feudally. Employment, housing and transport were all under the control of the laird, who could evict anyone at short notice. One owner, Schellenberg, claimed he wanted the keep the island with the 'slightly run-down … Hebridean feel'. When the islanders set up a trust to buy the island, he called them 'barmy revolutionaries' and claimed they weren't responsible enough to manage the land. In an example typical of his interactions with his tenants, he decided to remove an ancient map that had been part of the island's heritage for 200 years. However, the door to the building where the map was displayed had been inexplicably blocked by the community bus and apparently no-one could find the key.

The ingenuity of the islanders didn't pay off, as Schellenberg eventually got his hands on the map, but they did win the bigger battle. After a lot of hard work and donations from 10,000 members of the public, Eigg was bought in a three-way partnership between the islanders, the Highland Council and the Scottish Wildlife Trust. Of course, it is much easier to unite against a single problem than to unite for a concept, but over the following 25 years the islanders achieved a hugely successful transformation from feudalism to democracy. When we visit, their amazing achievements are all on show. The island is now self-sufficient in energy, having transitioned from generators running on imported diesel to a combined system of hydro, wind and solar power. This is the first scheme in the world to provide 24-hour green electricity. The population has risen to over 100 inhabitants.

Housing has been refurbished and is provided at affordable rents. Visitors are welcomed with spaces to camp, public showers and a café selling delicious food. They come to see otters, eagles, seals and the beautiful landscape, and this generates income and jobs.

My research into community land regeneration came full circle during the writing of this book, when the estate next to Tayvallich, where I live, came up for sale. Much of the land in Scotland is owned by absentee landlords of vast estates. As previously on Eigg, many rural inhabitants have no security of housing tenure, as they rent from the estate where they work. There is no benefit to estate-owners in selling properties to their employees. When Tayvallich Estate came on the market, locals were worried that the land would be parcelled up and asset-stripped. People's homes could be sold out from under them. Holiday houses in such a scenic location fetch a good price, one that most locals can't afford.

Our community didn't just sit around waiting to see what would be imposed on us next. We investigated a community land purchase, and this involved much research, discussion and a reimagining of what our community might be. Matters were resolved when the sellers of the estate gifted some land to the village in return for not bidding on the rest of the property, as a community buyout would prolong the sale. The majority of the estate was sold to a company called Highlands Rewilding, but the land near the village became the community-owned Tayvallich Initiative. And this is where the hard work started.

The long-term success of a community land-ownership project involves the unglamorous tasks of collaboration, compromise and sitting on committees. As one islander on Eigg told me, to make such a community work 'you need the dreamers and the grafters'. People who can afford the high property prices in rural locations are often retired people who have had a lifetime to earn or save enough money. But retired people might legitimately feel that they have done their grafting. To make positive change, we need to enable more young people to invest their energy and enthusiasm in our community. Land ownership gives

[opposite] *Resting eider ducks*

us the opportunity to build affordable housing to change our demographic. The arrival of the internet makes rural life more appealing for young people. Now it's possible to live in this beautiful location and still be connected for work or culture to the rest of the world. More families with children will keep our village school going. Land ownership also gives us local options to grow food, create jobs, generate electricity and increase biodiversity.

I've been inspired during the writing of this book by the huge range of solutions that communities have found to the problems of landscape degradation, biodiversity loss and global warming. I've also discovered that a project can start in many different ways. A community can be created and galvanised by the fight for a common cause, but change can be made in quieter ways too. The enthusiasm of just one person who sees a problem, and engages with their community, can have long-lasting effects. One such person is a friend, Mary-Lou Aitchison. She has started a wildlife club in our village for children aged between five and eleven. She is keen to point out to me that she's not any sort of expert. She does, however have huge energy. We meet at 10am, and she has already walked the dog, fed horses, made breakfast pancakes for her house-guests and answered a bunch of emails.

I join the club on the village playing field where they are pulling out the invasive weed, Himalayan balsam. The plant is head-high, but the roots are small, so it's a satisfying job, and the children seem to be loving it. As we work, we chat. Mary-Lou gets out her phone to read me a quote from David Attenborough. 'No-one will protect what they don't care about, and no-one will care about what they've never experienced.' This was her inspiration for the club. 'I want to give people good experiences, then they'll care,' she says.

The club has just returned from its summer camping trip to the island of Colonsay, with 33 adults and children. This was a massive organisational undertaking, and to make it happen, the support of the community was vital. People prepared food, lent camping equipment or contributed financially. It was important to Mary-Lou that everyone could take part, and so she did a sponsored walk to subsidise the trip. 'I was so surprised by how much I raised,' she says. 'I think it's because everyone knows that kids need to spend more time outdoors.' The village cake-makers were also co-opted. 'Lis Lawson's tablet kept us going,' she laughs.

The rest of the year, Mary-Lou organises monthly meetings, bringing in different experts to run, for example, moth-traps or make nest boxes. She doesn't mind if the children don't remember the names of the butterflies – she wants them to remember the experience. 'It's not a biology lesson and I'm not a teacher.'

She says it's important to build in lots of free time and let things develop. 'They are happy with very little.' Sometimes just learning how to go outside in the rain, or the fact that the tide comes in and out every day, is enough. 'Their lives have so much school and screens,' she says. Being out at unusual times of day is also revelatory. An early morning walk to listen to the dawn chorus, or a night-time survey of toads for the local nature reserve gives a fresh perspective on the world. Her highlight of the last field-trip was seeing a local farmer's daughter, inspired by a visit to an RSPB reserve, realise that farming and wildlife could go together. 'I am a very small cog in the wheel,' Mary-Lou tells me, 'but it feels right to be part of the turning and to leave the world in the well-prepared hands of the next generation.'

I find this project so exciting, partly because of its simplicity. It's something that many of us could make happen, but how many of us actually get on and do it? Inspiring the next generation is hugely valuable, but this project isn't expensive to run. It just needs time, enthusiasm and the support of a community.

Turnstones

Communities are made up of a tension between the needs of individuals and the group. In our own village, fishermen, farmers and conservationists all have different priorities, and finding solutions that suit everyone sometimes seems impossible. But because we will continue to meet each other in the pub or the village shop, we have to find a way. As I write this chapter I can see out in the garden a field scabious flower that is growing in our tiny lawn-meadow. The stem has grown unfeasibly tall, to reach above the competing grass. However, without these supporting grass stems all around it, the plant would soon snap in the wind. This balance of conflict and collaboration seems like a great analogy for community life.

Some of the projects in this book were born of conflict between two communities, as with the conservationists and farmers living with geese on Islay. Others were created by centuries of collaboration, like the crofting of machair in the Outer Hebrides. Some stories were as simple as Annette finding a dead swift stuck in her gutter and motivating her neighbours to install nest boxes. Some were complicated, like the multi-generational seabird research on St Kilda. Locations have been as small as a garden, or on a landscape scale, like the restoration of ancient woodland in Loch Arkaig, and the sea-grass regeneration in the Argyll Hope Spot. Some, like the whisky distillery on Harris, were started with the idea of one visionary person, but the success of the project came when the community engaged with the idea to give it a long-term future.

Interviewees sometimes confided to me that the charismatic movers and shakers, who felt passionately enough to galvanise a whole movement, were not always those best suited to manage the project once the initial victories had been achieved. The baton had to be passed to those who could do the less exciting, but no less valuable, work of form-filling and fundraising.

Some of the projects involved land purchases, as in the Peatland chapter, but others, as in the Coast chapter, involved a moral rather than legal ownership. This chimes with a traditional view of our west coast landscape. Dan the Merman told me that in Gaelic the concept of ownership only refers linguistically to body parts, your spirit, thoughts, and close or intimate people. 'People belong to places, but places don't belong to people,' he said.

One of the questions I posed at the start of this book was whether we still needed the natural world. I've come to the conclusion that as well as providing our life support system, nature can have the same function as a religion. It's a way of being part of something bigger than ourselves; it's here when we're born and will continue after we're gone. It inspires a sense of awe, with its complexity and beauty. It puts our own lives into perspective whilst providing a framework where we can find our place. It also offers a type of immortality; all the elements in our bodies were once part of other living beings, and will be once again in the future. In writing this book I've realised that I could say many of those same things about community. It's a structure that is more than the sum of its parts. It provides a role that gives meaning to life. Although sitting at a committee table does, at times, make one lose the will to live, community allows us to achieve more. It can even offer an afterlife if that appeals, when other people continue the work that we have started and remember what we have achieved.

When I look back at the adjectives that I used to describe the people I met in this book, 'enthusiastic' was one of the most common. It's clear that people who take action, rather than bemoaning the state of the world, benefit emotionally. By using their skills to make change, they are regaining some agency. It's indisputable that the natural world faces huge problems. Some days the threats of global warming and biodiversity loss seem to me insurmountable. As my husband Mark says, 'watching the news makes you feel disempowered, impotent and distraught.' However, dejection is not a very useful emotion, and it doesn't spur us on to make change. On the other hand, I don't want the stories in this book to leave readers feeling complacent that other people are solving all the problems of the natural world. I hope instead, that the examples of these amazing people will provide inspiration for the question 'What can I do?' or even better, 'What can we do?'

ACKNOWLEDGEMENTS

The saying 'It takes a village to raise a child' could equally apply to the writing of this book. Appropriately, it has been a community effort, from its conception and birth, to the feeding and clothing of it. Many of the contributors have already been named in the text, and they deserve the most gratitude. Without their generosity in sharing stories, this book would still be a toddler, stumbling around inside my head and spilling breakfast cereal on the floor.

Commissioning editor, Hugh Andrew at Birlinn, believed in the potential of my child, and paid for its education. The book's big-boy-cousin was Rowan Aitchison, who read some of the text, and with youthful enthusiasm, encouraged it in new directions. The wise aunties were my book group, who nurtured my writing abilities.

The Artmap Argyll Open Studio Trail has provided the equivalent of High School. Every year in August, with fellow artists across Argyll, I welcome the public into my studio. The many wonderful conversations that I've had with visitors over the years has informed my artwork and also introduced me to new mentors.

And then there were the field trips. I'm an elected member of the Society of Wildlife Artists. Most of us work outside, and seeing the grit of those who paint in wind and rain or when the colours are freezing on the paper, is inspiring. Their website gives an idea of the range of talent that has inspired me to be braver with my artwork.

When this book became a teenager and needed to take a driving test and get an ISBN, the responsible adults stepped in. Tom Johnstone, editor of my first book, *Wild Island*, proof-read the text. Nye Hughes went above and beyond on the design. Andrew Simmons, Editorial Manager at Birlinn, tutored my awkward offspring through all its exams.

My husband, Mark, has been the perfect co-parent. When things got difficult he cooked dinner and gave encouragement. My human children provided technical support with social media. And now it's time for the book to make its own way in the big wide world. I'll miss it being around every day, but will be glad of more time to work at my printmaking. I hope we can meet up regularly, at book festivals or talks. I'm looking forward to it bringing new friends home, so I can continue to learn about the exciting possibilities of Community.

JS 2025